THE SURVIVAL HANDBOOK FOR EVERYONE

pil

Publications International, Ltd.

Written by Jim Daley

Images from Shutterstock.com

ISBN: 978-1-64030-648-6

Manufactured in China.

8 7 6 5 4 3 2 1

This publication is only intended to provide general information. The information
is specifically not intended to be substitute for medical diagnosis or treatment by
your physician or other healthcare professional. You should always consult your own
physician or other healthcare professionals about any medical questions, diagnosis,
or treatment. (Products vary among manufacturers. Please check labels carefully to
confirm that the products you use are appropriate for your condition.)

The information obtained by you from this publication should not be relied upon for any
personal, nutritional, or medical decision. You should consult an appropriate professional
for specific advice tailored to your specific situation. PIL makes no representation or
warranties, express or implied, with respect to your use of this information.

In no event shall PIL or its affiliates or advertisers be liable for any direct, indirect,
punitive, incidental, special, or consequential damages, or any damages whatsoever
including, without limitation, damages for personal injury, death, damage to property
or loss of profits, arising out of or in any way connected with the use of any of the
above-referenced information or otherwise arising out of use of this publication.

TABLE OF CONTENTS

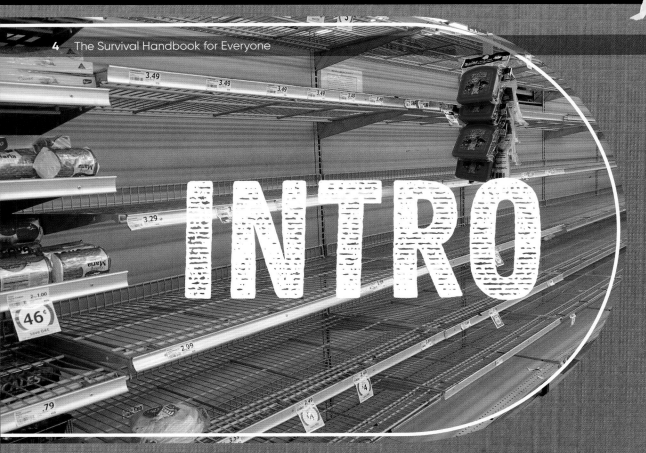

INTRO

Stores can quickly sell out of standard items as people prepare for hurricanes.

Most families who live in North America don't know how much they depend on outside services for their survival. We depend on the store for our food and daily living supplies. We are surrounded by technology that gives us all of our information and much of our entertainment. Gadgets store and cook our food and keep our houses warm in the winter and cool in the summer. We have a sense of security in our houses and cities. We think our appliances will always work. We expect the government to bail us out in the face of a crisis. We think that our access to food and supplies will never be threatened. Nothing could be further from the truth.

Keeping your fridge stocked depends on transportation networks and computerized inventory control. When there is a run on

grocery stores supplies are unavailable after just a few hours. We take for granted that we will have continued access to medical care. But this is usually one of the first systems that fail in an emergency. We're dependent on our credit or debit cards. We're not ready unprepared if the ATM on the corner abruptly stops working.

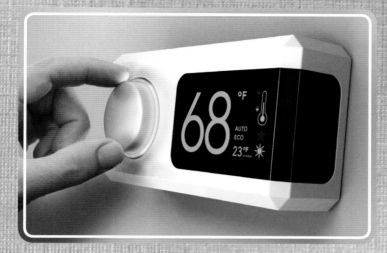

GADGETS CONTROL OUR HOMES. WHAT HAPPENS IF THE GADGETS STOP WORKING?

Yet the idea of being prepared for a crisis is one that many people see as strange. We think "preppers" are pessimistic or insecure. But the opposite is true. Preparing your family to survive a crisis will make you more secure. It will provide you with a feeling of calm in the face of a dire situation. Relying on yourself will let you deal with tough circumstances. You'll understand them for what they are: a challenge, not a catastrophe.

A first aid kit and savings will prepare you for an emergency. If you have a woodpile or a vegetable garden, you are somewhat independent from the grid. Owning a flashlight and a smoke detector helps prepare for emergencies. Planning for a crisis just takes these kinds of actions a step or two further. Preparation doesn't take much. It means storing food for your family. It means knowing what your needs are in a crisis. And it means stocking supplies that can help you get through a crisis. These are all sensible safety measures. History has shown us that crises strike more often than we would like.

This guide will show you how to prepare yourself to survive a crisis. It may be a major power outage that lasts more than a few days. It may be an extreme weather event that makes leaving your house untenable. You may have to survive civil unrest. The skills and advice in this book will help you survive. All it takes is some simple preparations and stocking a few basic supplies. We live in a world that is unstable. There are multiple threats, from the problem of global warming and extreme weather events, to disease, terrorist attacks, and food insecurity. Our systems of transportation, finance, and communications are fragile. And most Americans are only a few days away from going hungry. By knowing the skills to be self-reliant, you will be prepared if the worst happens.

Being prepared can give you and your family comfort.

CHAPTER 1:
15 RULES TO FOLLOW

RULE 1: PREPARE MENTALLY

Being mentally ready is critical to survival. There are several ways of being mentally prepared for surviving. You have to know what to expect. Memorize a plan of action. Have a skill set that will keep you alive. And keep your morale up in the face of a crisis. By preparing yourself ahead of time, you will have much better chances. You'll be able to keep your wits about you. This way, you'll react the right way to a crisis. That means staying calm. This is key to surviving a crisis wherever you are.

PREPARATION IS KEY

Staying calm depends on how prepared you are mentally to deal with a crisis. Soldiers talk about how training "kicks in" in the heat of battle. This lets them work in the face of extreme difficulty. If you are properly trained for an emergency, you will be far less likely to panic. That means having a plan. It also means practicing the plan until you have it memorized. Your training should focus on worst-case scenarios. This way, you are prepared for the most difficult circumstances. But it will also make it much easier to deal with less stressful emergencies.

KEEP UP MORALE

After the initial crisis, you may have to deal with its outcomes for some time. Emergency services may not be able to help you. Civil authorities may lose control and be forced to abandon your area altogether. And if you're stuck in a remote area, search and rescue may take days to find you. This is when keeping up morale over the long term is very important.

It's easy to fall into despair after several days in survival mode. This is very real when there's no resolution in sight. Even if you are not in immediate physical danger, you'll be dealing with elevated levels of stress. Over time this can take its toll. You will not be sleeping as much as you are used to. Food and water have to be rationed. You won't be able to enjoy showering or changing your clothes regularly. Members of your party may be injured or dead.

STICK TO A ROUTINE

The best way to keep up morale is to make sure everyone has assigned responsibilities. Have a routine and stick to it. Give members of your party a set amount of tasks they need to take care of each day. This will help focus them. And it will keep their minds off of more stressful thoughts. Human beings psychologically crave routine. A survival situation is a huge disruption to their normal lives. This is why it's important to get back on a set routine as soon as possible. Mentally prepare yourself and your family for this. Figure out each person's role in the event of a crisis. Practice them at least twice a year.

SET GOALS

If you are alone, set a list of tasks for each day. This includes finding water and foraging for food. You'll also have to build or repair shelter. Get your bearings and scout the immediate area for threats or survivors. If you are in a group, divide tasks among the group members according to skill level and physical ability. It's important that people feel they are liable to the rest of the group. This helps bond the group together and keep up morale. Pay attention to the attitudes of individual group members. Intervene if anyone seems like they may be overly stressed or heading for a breakdown.

Repairing a fishing net

PRACTICE AND PREPARE

Again, all of this is much easier if you have worked out and practiced a survival plan. The more prepared you are for any emergency, the better your chances of surviving it, physically and emotionally.

RULE 2: ASSESS THE SITUATION

Determining the nature of the crisis is very important to surviving it. There are various kinds of crises that can occur, and each of them carries a different threat level and urgency. The type of crisis also will determine your reaction to it. An outbreak of disease will necessitate a different response than an extreme weather event. However, with the right stock of supplies and the correct mental preparedness, you will be ready to respond to a range of different crises quickly.

LOW OR HIGH INTENSITY?

Certain crises will be low-intensity, such as a long term power outage or moderately severe weather event. These kinds of crises, for the most part, only require you to have a store of supplies that can keep you warm and dry and prevent you from going hungry if the situation lasts more than a few days. Other crises will be high-intensity and present an emergent threat, such as major civil unrest or a particularly extreme weather event. These kinds of crises will require you to assess whether there is an immediate threat to your family's safety and the security of your home, and if it is high, to decide when and how to leave the area.

Downed power lines may lead to a prolonged outage.

EXAMPLES OF LOW-INTENSITY CRISIS:

• A major blizzard that city officials are unable to respond to right away, shutting down transportation, causing businesses to close, and stranding you at home. You'll need to have enough nonperishable food and water to last for the duration of the crisis, and your ability to cook or even heat your home may be affected.

• A regional power outage that lasts for several days, resulting in looting of business districts and making the streets unsafe at night. Any perishable food will quickly go bad, but with enough backup supplies, you should be able to shelter at home and wait for power to be restored.

• A terrorist attack on your city's financial district that results in a citywide shutdown of businesses, interruption of public transit services, or security-related shutdowns of highways and bridges. The security of your home is not threatened, but you may not want to—or be able to—go about your normal routine for a few days.

EXAMPLES OF HIGH-INTENSITY CRISIS:

• An extreme weather event such as a major hurricane, which can knock out power, communications, and other utilities; flood low-lying areas; and directly impact the structural integrity of buildings, including your home.

Hurricanes like Harvey wrought extreme destruction.

• Serious civil unrest, during which civil authorities cede control of whole sections of the city to rioters or looters, who may set fires and destroy private property. The civil unrest may be occurring in a different area of the city, or it may be approaching your neighborhood.

• An outbreak of highly communicable, deadly disease that overwhelms medical facilities and makes contact with other people very risky. Sheltering indoors is safe if you can seal off most of your house and have supplies for a few weeks, but evacuation is risky because of elevated exposure to others, who may be carriers.

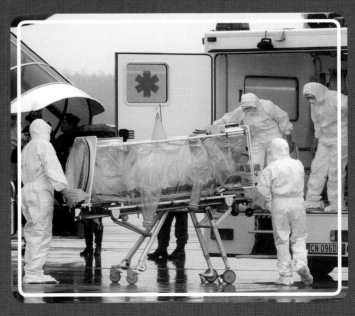

RULE 3: HAVE WHAT YOU NEED

There are a number of items that are critical to surviving virtually any kind of crisis. You will need shelter from the elements, several days' or weeks' worth of food and water, and first aid supplies at the very minimum. There are also a number of useful tools that you will want to have immediately after a situation occurs. These include one or more communications devices, several flashlights, and basic survival gear.

WATER

Regardless of whether you are dealing with a short term crisis or one that will likely stretch on for several weeks or months, having potable water is essential. Going without water more than a few days is not survivable. Make sure you have enough water on hand for every member of your household to drink for at least a week's time. You should already have bottled water among your emergency supplies, but augment it by filling any available sealable containers with tap water. Additionally, if you are experiencing a long-term power outage during winter months, keep your faucets running to prevent your pipes from freezing.

FOOD

Make sure you have a nonperishable food supply. It is critical to your survival. You should have enough energy bars, trail mix, and other ready-to-eat food to last at least three days. Having enough for a week is better. Whether you are evacuating or sheltering at home, you need enough food that you won't have to worry about it. This allows you to spend your time and energy on other tasks.

FIRST AID

During a crisis, two factors greatly increase the degree to which you will have to be self-reliant for medical care. First, hospitals and other medical facilities are not designed to deal with the influx of patients that occurs with any crisis. In a very short amount of time, hospitals soon have to go into triage mode; when this is the case, patients with minor wounds may find themselves waiting days for medical care, if they get any. Second, during a crisis, your odds of being wounded or injured are higher than they are normally. This is true regardless of the nature of the crisis. Because of your elevated risk of injury and the likelihood that hospitals may not be able to help you, it's very important to have a first aid kit that you can use to treat most injuries as well as the skill set to know what to do with it.

OTHER SURVIVAL GEAR

While food, water, and medical supplies are the most critical items to ensuring your ability to survive a crisis, there are a number of other things you'll also need, whether you are sheltering at home or evacuating. Your "bug out" bag will contain food, water, and medical supplies. It will also need to be equipped with supplies you can use to make shelter, build a fire, navigate roads leading to safety, defend yourself, and keep warm and dry. In the event that you do have to evacuate, a properly equipped bug out bag is essential to ensuring that you have everything you need to survive the evacuation within minutes of making the decision to go. For more information about what goes in your bug out bag, see pages 21–23 and 56–59.

RULE 4: STAY INFORMED

Assessing your situation—and doing so in the early stages of the crisis—is key to ensuring you are able to react and make survival decisions quickly and in enough time for them to be effective. In order to ensure that you have uninterrupted access to regular news reports whether or not you have electricity or access to a television, keep a hand-crank/solar-powered radio in your emergency supplies. These radios let you to be independent of batteries or wall power. Solar-powered models charge themselves continuously, and a hand-crank option is excellent when you cannot go outside.

GET NEWS

Additional options for obtaining—and sharing—news and information include emergency band scanners, CB radios, and emergency alert radios. Emergency band scanners will let you to listen directly to communications between police, firefighters, paramedics, and public safety officers. CB radios do not have a lot of range, but they are a useful way to keep track of local conditions and communicate with other people. They can be particularly useful for communicating while you are on the road.

KEEP TRACK

As soon as a crisis situation starts to develop, make sure that a member of your party is continually monitoring the radio, and if it is still available, watching television news reports. Keep a detailed log book of the reports you receive. This lets you to make better decisions based on real-time information: If it's written down, it can't be forgotten or easily overlooked, and you can track the degree of severity as the crisis develops. This way, you'll know right away what you should do.

KNOW WHAT'S HAPPENING

While you do not have to follow the directives provided by emergency broadcasts, it's important to be aware of what local, state, and federal governments are advising citizens to do during a crisis. You want to know whether emergency broadcasts are directing people to evacuate an area or shelter at home. In the event of natural crises, such as severe storms or fast-moving wildfires, it will be critical to keep abreast of developments and know whether the natural event (fires, flooding) is moving your way—this way you'll know whether you need to get out before it is too late to do so.

KNOW WHAT TO DO WITH THE INFORMATION

If you have already prepared yourself and your family for a range of different crises, you will be much better equipped to digest the information in emergency broadcasts and news reports and make decisions quickly. You'll already know which emergencies mean you should button up your house and prepare to shelter on your own for a short while, and which ones mean you should immediately evacuate. And because you'll be more prepared than most of your neighbors, you'll be able to react to the crisis more quickly than they can. This will help you to avoid either being stuck in a miles-long traffic jam or left scrounging empty supermarket shelves for supplies during a run on a grocery store. While your unprepared neighbors are dealing with one of those situations, you and your family will already be long gone or comfortably hunkered down with plenty of food and supplies.

RULE 5: HAVE A PLAN FOR CIVIL UNREST

Civil unrest describes a broad category of general lawlessness that can accompany another crisis. It can also occur without a larger crisis as a spark. It can be started by anger at civil authorities over politically motivated reasons. Or it can even grow out of rioting inspired by something as trivial as a national sports title. Civil unrest is dangerous because it is unpredictable and can grow quickly. Within 24 hours, police and civil authorities can lose control of whole neighborhoods. Residents and business owners will be on their own to protect their lives and property.

BE ORGANIZED

Being prepared is the best way to survive any crisis. Civil unrest is no exception. You'll need supplies and evacuation/sheltering plans of action. You should also develop a network of trusted friends or like-minded survivalists. With a group you can work together to survive the event. It will be easier to defend yourselves from looters and rioters if you are organized. Rioters typically are spontaneous and disorganized. They rely on the cover of the mob for their actions. The cure for this is an organized, well-prepared group with a plan of action and preset roles.

HAVE A PLAN

Telephone lines are easily overwhelmed during civil unrest. It's very important to have a set plan for meeting up with other members of your group that does not rely on cell phones. You can communicate with one another via CB radio or walkie-talkies. But these devices have limited range. They're also not secure, so others could be listening in. You also may not be able to access your radio in the initial hours of civil unrest. Therefore every member of your party should know where they need to go to meet up. It can be at your home or another prearranged location.

SHELTER AT HOME?

If civil unrest is not occurring in your area, it may be best to shelter at home with other members of your group for the time being. You should have a solid security plan and lock down your home. That can allow you to ride out the civil unrest until the situation is under control. But the rioting and/or looting will pose a serious threat to your area. Or the civil unrest may too widespread for authorities to contain. When that happens get out of the city.

SHOULD YOU EVACUATE?

Evacuation has the best chance of success early in a crisis. Get out fast. Avoid being stuck within a miles-long traffic jam. By getting out fast you avoid this kind of situation and the problems that go with it. You may not be able to escape unrest by car. Be prepared to walk out of your city. Map out prearranged escape routes. This way you can avoid the areas where rioting is going on.

KEEP YOUR DISTANCE

You may find yourself in the vicinity of looters or rioters. When that happens, you need to put as much distance between you and them as you can. Keep a low profile. Try to avoid being seen. Don't wear anything that is valuable enough to attract attention. Move quickly away from rioters. And once you're in a safer area, assess how you can get to the meet up spot from there.

RULE 6: BE READY TO LEAVE

Knowing when you should bug out is nearly as critical as having a well-prepared bug out bag. In any crisis, the best time to evacuate is always going to be before the event reaches a critical point. The critical point could be one of many things. It may be an extreme weather event that makes travel impossible. Or it could be a period of civil unrest that makes travel dangerous. Or it may just be the point at which so many people are evacuating that roads are impassable. But when it occurs, it will be much more difficult to get out. It's better to be safe than sorry. So unless you are prepared to shelter at home for the long term, getting out earlier is always better. You can always return in a few days if the crisis does not develop into a more severe or long-term event.

KEEP A BUG OUT BAG

Every member of your household should have their own bug out bag. This is a backpack that has enough supplies to survive for a minimum of 72 hours. Each bug out bag should contain enough supplies for the individual to be well equipped to survive even if they become separated from the rest of the group. In addition to this, you can spread backup and additional supplies around everyone's bug out bags. This is a way of extending your survival ability. No one person should be responsible for any backup supply. This prevents the group from losing access to valuable items should one person lose their bag or be unable to get to it before you evacuate.

STOCK YOUR BAG

• At least 3 liters of water, and plenty of iodine tablets for water purification.

• Nonperishable, lightweight, high-protein food supplies, MREs, energy bars, and trail mix are all excellent options. Dehydrated camping meals are also very good to have.

• Hiking boots and at least one change of clothes, including extra pairs of socks and underwear, cold weather clothing, heavy duty poncho, and leather gloves.

• Reflective emergency survival blanket and a 6 x 10 foot nylon tarp.

• Basic first aid kit.

• Small, 30–40 degree sleeping bag.

• Prepared tinder and at least three ways to start fire, such as butane lighters, all-weather matches in a waterproof container, and fire steel.

• A knife and multi-tool.

• Flashlights and extra batteries. LED flashlights are particularly good because they are bright, are available as headlamps, and do not drain batteries quickly.

• Communications devices, including a fully charged cell phone, a hand-crank emergency AM/FM radio, and walkie-talkie.

• Important documents, including identification, medical information, important phone numbers, and firearm carry permit.

• Maps of the city, state, and region and a compass.

• Self-defense items. What you choose to carry is up to you, but you should have a self-defense item that you can use to engage hostile individuals at a distance, such as pepper spray, a taser, or a firearm. Avoiding hand-to-hand combat is very important. But you should also carry a backup weapon such as a baton or heavy flashlight for that eventuality.

GOOD TO HAVE

These additional items are also useful to augment the basic bug out bag:

- Lightweight camping tent and lightweight wool blanket.

- Additional food supplies, including canned meats and beans.

- Cash—at least $500.

- Toilet paper.

- 200 feet of paracord or nylon rope.

- Dust masks with filters.

- Personal hygiene supplies such as toothbrush/toothpaste, soap, hand sanitizer, etc.

- Binoculars.

- Small sewing kit.

- Whistle and small mirror for communication with other group members at short distances.

- GPS devices.

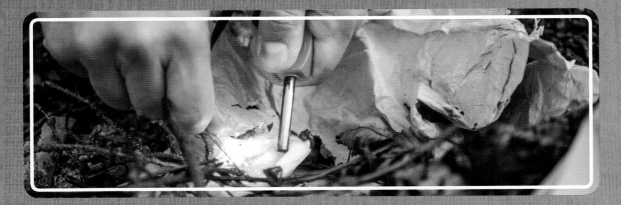

**Don't forget pools as a
source of water.**

RULE 7: HAVE A WATER PLAN

Water is essential to your survival. Even if you have a good supply of it, during a crisis, you will not want to rely on just your stored water. You cannot rely on tap water. It can become contaminated even if it's still running. Have your gutters connect to rain barrels. This way you can collect rainwater for your garden and household use. Make sure you are equipped with the tools and skills to purify water. And learn where you can forage for water.

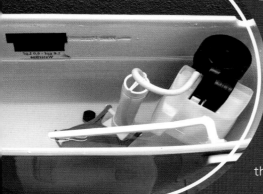

IN THE HOUSE

In a city, there are many places to find water. The fact is that houses are full of water. When you are looking in a house, there are two key reservoirs you can check. Look for hot water heaters in the basement. These will often be able to provide all the water you can carry. Next on the list are toilet tanks. The water in toilet tanks is the same water from the tap. Most toilet tanks have 1–3 gallons of water in them. Older houses will have steam radiators. You can drain several gallons from them, depending on their size.

IN THE NEIGHBORHOOD

Also check for gutters connected to rain barrels or reservoirs. When you find them, remember where they are. You'll be able to revisit them any time it rains. If the water main has been shut off, you can drain the water in apartment buildings' pipes. Find the lowest faucet in the building, and allow gravity to do the work. As you travel, keep an eye out for aboveground pools. They may be chlorinated or dirty, but you can treat the water.

AROUND TOWN

Office parks are an overlooked source for scavenging water. Many large office buildings will have water reservoirs on the roof. You can often access the roof by the fire escape. They hold hundreds of gallons, so you can use them over and over. Office buildings also usually have dozens of spare, full water cooler tanks. They hold 3–5 gallons. They're also sealed, fresh, and very portable.

PURIFICATION

Once you have water, you need to purify it. There are three basic methods for purifying water: disinfecting it with bleach or iodine, distilling it, or filtering it. Boiling water, if you have the resources available to do so, has pros and cons. While it is cheap, fast, and reliable, it can wind up using a lot of valuable fuel that you may not be able to spare.

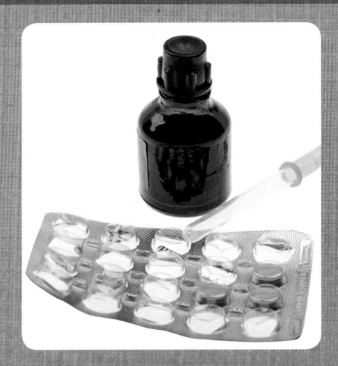

DISINFECTANTS

Disinfecting with chlorine or iodine is not quite as effective as boiling. Disinfecting with chlorine or iodine is dependent on water temperature and pH; generally, they are most effective in warm water with a neutral pH (7.0). Chlorine is simply household bleach, while iodine is available at most pharmacies. Add eight drops of bleach per gallon of water. Stir it briskly and let it to sit for at least an hour. Iodine works best with smaller quantities of water. Use three drops of 2% iodine solution per quart of clear water, and twice as much if the water is cold or cloudy. Stir it briskly and let it sit for half an hour.

FILTERS

A mechanical filter or distiller is best when you are very concerned about your water supply. These are available as small, pocket-sized models designed for a bug out bag to larger systems that can supply your whole house with clean water. Portable water filters typically need the filter to be replaced after 100 gallons, but they have the advantage that they are easy to store and carry to water sources if your tap stops working or your well runs dry.

Reverse osmosis filters are expensive and take up a fair amount of counter space, but they provide you with extremely pure water. The main drawback to these filters is that they have to be hooked up to your water line; they will not work without some water flow. Tabletop water filters are effective, can be used with any water supply, and require no electricity. Larger units can hold several gallons of water and filter up to four gallons per hour. They are not particularly portable, but are excellent for home use.

DISTILLERS

Distillation is the process of boiling water and letting the steam condense and collect in a storage container. A good distiller can process up to sixteen gallons of water per day. They do not require electricity, but do need a fair amount of fuel to keep the water boiling. A distiller can cost up to several hundred dollars, but ensures you will have a sustainable supply of safe water in the event of shortages.

RULE 8: HAVE A FOOD PLAN

Having access to food sources is very important to long-term survival, particularly in the kind of crisis that cuts off transportation and distribution networks for a period of several weeks or months. While you may be able to access grocery stores in the initial hours of the crisis, they will quickly become overwhelmed and should not be considered a reliable source of food. That is why it is imperative that you have enough stored, nonperishable food in your house to last for several weeks.

DRY FOOD SUPPLIES

This includes stores of dry food supplies. Rice and beans are particularly useful storage foods for the long term: They last practically indefinitely and are very easy to prepare. It is also highly recommended that you keep a supply of canned food in your survival stock. The fact is, you can keep enough canned and dried food to last you several months in a relatively small space. A few shelving units in your basement or pantry can hold enough food to let you to survive comfortably. But what about when you are dealing with a long-term situation such as economic or government collapse?

GROW YOUR OWN

In this situation, it's best to be self-reliant. This means having the ability to produce food in and around your home, as doing so will let you to take care of your family's needs in normal times and during a crisis. This is where a backyard, rooftop, or patio garden can be very useful. It may not be able to take the place of all trips to the local grocery store, or meet all of your family's food needs during a crisis. But learning to grow some of your own food will reduce your dependence on a food distribution system that will break down without electricity or fossil fuels.

SUPPLEMENT YOUR FOOD STORES

While your goal should not be to have a totally self contained homestead in the middle of the city, you can still organize your home and property to be fairly self-reliant during a crisis. Your garden can supplement your stored food supplies, which will let it last much longer and add fresh variety to your diet. And your garden can even supplement your food stores: by canning, drying, pickling, or otherwise preserving your vegetables for long-term storage, you can have a well-stocked food supply that can help you be more self-sufficient.

URBAN GARDENS

Take stock of the available space around your home and property. You'll be surprised at the number of vegetables you can grow even if you live in an apartment building. Your rooftop can support dozens of vegetables in containers. You can grow plenty of vegetables on your patio or back porch, and use windowsills to grow herbs and greens. A trellis in your backyard can support beans and peas. And one or two raised beds in your backyard can grow many pounds of vegetables for eating or storage.

COMMUNITY GARDENS

Chances are there is also a community garden space in your neighborhood. Talk to the people who garden there, and see about getting your own plot to work. This is not only in order to give yourself a bit of extra gardening space. Joining a community garden is an important way to build community with like-minded neighbors. You can learn valuable gardening tips, exchange seeds, and in times of crisis, help one another out.

SMALL LIVESTOCK

Most urban municipalities allow homeowners to keep a few chickens on their property. To do so, all they require is that you obtain a permit and build a proper chicken coop to house them. Some municipalities even let you keep rabbits or goats as well. If you decide to turn your backyard into something of an urban homestead, and keep a few small livestock, you will be practically entirely self-sufficient. Eggs, goat's milk, and rabbit meat can not only keep you well supplied with protein and dairy year round, but can also be valuable bartering items to obtain supplies.

SMALL GAME

Cities are also chock-full of game. Most people don't know it, but there's a reason cities are full of pigeons. For centuries people kept pigeons in cities as a food source. We no longer do, but the pigeons stayed. These birds are surprisingly meaty. And young pigeons are even a delicacy called squab. Because urban pigeons are also tame, they're easy to hunt. You can get within a few yards of a pigeon. And it won't be disturbed by your presence. Squirrels are also abundant in many cities and fairly tame. Other cities have feral rabbits and possums. In Detroit, there are feral peacocks! Most of these animals are very used to humans' presence, so you can get very close to them. That will make them much easier to shoot or trap than wild game. Learn about the feral animals in your city, and where to look for them.

HUNTING

With a small-caliber rifle, or even an air rifle and good aim, you can shoot a pigeon or squirrel. If you don't have a firearm, there are other options. You can build a slingshot or bow and arrows very easily with scavenged material. With some practice, you will have a good enough aim that you'll be able to shoot small game from twenty yards or less. If you get a firearm or bow and arrows now, you can have the skills you need before the crisis.

TRAPPING

An alternative to shooting game is trapping it. While shooting it takes less patience, you will use up bullets and may even attract unwanted attention. There are many simple traps you can make. The easiest one just needs a box, a long string, and a stick. Tie the string around the stick. Place the box on an angle resting on the stick. Put some bait under the box. The bait depends on the game you're hunting. Know what the feral game in your city like to eat. Then, you just wait for your game to walk into the trap, and pull the string, dropping the box on top of it.

SCAVENGE PLANTS

There is a good chance that your city has many edible plants. Many weeds are quite edible. Dandelions, thistles, garlic mustard, bee balm, and mallow are all common edible weeds. Learn to identify them so you can recognize them when you're scavenging. Many cities also have fruit trees and bushes. Wild grapes, mulberry trees, apple trees, or citrus trees are present in many cities. Learn where they are in your area. You should have a plant identification guide. This way you can find out whether unfamiliar plants are edible. But do so carefully.

Between growing your own food, hunting feral game and foraging for edible plants, you can live off the land for a long time. You should also store dried food. But it should be a last resort. Sustainable sources of food are better. And even in cities, they are everywhere.

RULE 9: TAKE CARE OF YOUR HEALTH

During a crisis, you will not be able to rely on emergency services when a medical emergency occurs. You may have to deal with any number of medical emergencies, from serious illnesses to broken bones or wounds. As with other aspects of survival, the best plan is to be properly prepared to deal with all of them. This involves having the proper skills and supplies.

FIRST AID KIT

Your first aid kit should be well stocked to deal with a range of different medical emergencies, and have enough supplies to last you for at least six months. You can purchase an assembled first aid kit and augment it with whatever additional supplies you may need. Your first aid kid should, at the very least, contain all of the following items:

- Hydrogen peroxide
- Rubbing alcohol
- Antibiotic ointment
- 1% cortisone cream
- Anti-diarrhea, anti-nausea, and antacid remedies
- Antihistamine
- Pain medication, such as ibuprofen, acetaminophen, and aspirin
- Toothache remedy
- Cough and cold medicine
- Thermometer
- Small and large adhesive bandages
- Small and large gauze pads

- First aid tape
- Butterfly closures
- Elastic bandages
- Slings and splints
- Instant hot/cold packs
- Cotton balls
- Tweezers, safety pins, small scissors
- Suture kit
- Sanitary napkins (which double as pressure bandages)
- Disposable latex gloves
- Electrolyte replacement therapy

Keep one first aid kit at your home and another in each of your cars. It's important to not just have the kits but also know exactly how to use them.

TRAINING FIRST

That means that you should enroll in a good first aid and CPR class as part of preparing for a crisis. Taking first-responder classes can be more expensive and time consuming, but can mean the difference between life and death for yourself or a loved one. All family members, including children, should be taught at least basic first aid. Keep a health care handbook or copy of the *Red Cross First Aid & Emergency Preparedness Quick Reference Guide* with your home first aid kit.

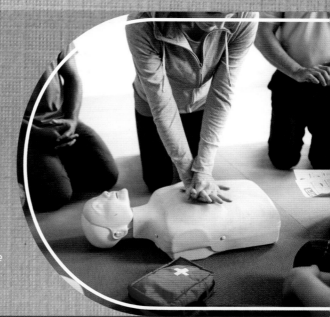

POOLING RESOURCES

As with other supplies, medical emergencies during a crisis can be made much more survivable if you have already established a sense of community with your neighbors. Chances are at least someone in your area is a medical professional or first responder. Tell them that you are taking first aid classes and why, and make sure you can rely on one another for help in the event of a crisis. The more you and your neighbors get to know one another, the easier it will be to establish support networks during a crisis.

RULE 10: KEEP IT CLEAN

Staying clean is as important to your long-term survival as food and shelter. If you don't keep yourself clean, you expose yourself not only to discomfort but to illness. Of course, during a long-term crisis you may not be able to enjoy a hot shower on a regular basis, but that doesn't mean you can't take basic steps to maintain your sanitation and personal hygiene. You can wash your entire body with just a bit of soap and a couple of cups of water. Plan on doing so at least every other day as circumstances allow. You should be ready to maintain your personal hygiene on the road as well as at home.

OPTIONS FOR WASTE DISPOSAL

If you are sheltering at home for an indeterminate time, and water pressure drops significantly, you may not be able to use your toilet. There are different options for how to prepare for this. If you have a backyard garden, the best solution is to purchase or build a composting toilet for disposing of your solid waste. Composting toilets turn solid waste into nutrient-rich fertilizer that is safe to spread on your garden, and they do not require a water supply to work. Buying a composting toilet can cost more than $1500, but they are dependable and provide fast, odorless decomposition. Alternately you can dig a "humanure" compost pit. Instruction manuals for building a long-term, sustainable "humanure" pit are available, and they can be built for a few hundred dollars or less.

SIMPLE WASTE DISPOSAL

The most straightforward alternative to either of these options is to use a large bucket with a heavy-duty plastic bag liner. Keep the bucket in the garage or shed for odor control. You can mount a regular toilet seat on the bucket for comfort. Keep a snap-on lid to control odor and flies. When the bag is full, bury it as deeply as possible, far from your house.

WASHING CLOTHES

One of the biggest challenges in the hygiene and sanitation category during a crisis is washing your clothes without power. Consider buying a washboard or plunger that you can use to clean clothes in your bathtub. Drying can be made much easier with a hand wringer: Wringing out your clothes is the toughest part of washing them by hand. A good wringer costs between $100 and $200, but it will be well worth the investment if you are wringing out heavy denim jeans or a dozen cloth diapers. You can hang clothes to dry in your yard, on your roof, or even in your home, depending on the weather.

RULE 11: PREPARE FOR PEOPLE

There is one thing that makes a survival situation in a city far more dangerous than in other areas. That is the high density of people. Cities are filled with people who are not at all prepared to survive a crisis, and this can make conditions very unsafe very quickly. This is why being fully prepared for a crisis is extremely important in a city. It's also why you should own and be trained to use at least one weapon that you keep in your house. While you hopefully will not need to use it, it's always better to be prepared.

STEER CLEAR OF STRANGERS

The best way to deal with strangers during a crisis is to avoid them altogether. As far as you can, stay away from areas where they are likely to congregate. This includes hospitals, grocery stores, pharmacies, and highways. You have two options during a crisis. You can shelter at home or evacuate. If you choose to stay, make sure you have enough supplies on hand well before the crisis begins. And be ready to fend off intruders.

EVACUATE SAFELY

If you choose to evacuate, avoid any major highways, bridges or tunnels as best you can. Use surface streets, service roads, and back roads to get out of the city. You may have no choice but to take one of a few major routes out of the city. When that is the case, do so as soon as possible. The risk of evacuating early is lower than the risk of evacuating too late. You want to avoid being stuck on the roads if they're clogged with people trying to escape. If evacuating by car is unsafe, you can walk or bicycle out of the city. Again, there may only be a few options for evacuation points. Some cities have choke points. Manhattan is an island. San Francisco is a peninsula. Learn the train lines, hiking trails, and side roads out of your city. That way you can walk out while avoiding most people.

KNOW YOUR NEIGHBORS

Most of the people who live in your area are not going to be dangerous. And some can even be helpful. The best way to ensure that your neighbors are sources of assistance and not danger is to get to know them. Make friends with them well before the onset of a crisis. It's very important to establish relationships with people who can help during a crisis. Together you can establish a neighborhood watch to protect your block. You can set up communication networks and work together to survive by pooling resources and skills.

BUILD A NETWORK

However, make sure that the people who know you are a "Prepper" can be trusted. You do want to establish friendships with your neighbors so you can rely on one another in difficult times. But you don't want the wrong people to know you have food, supplies, and weapons in your home. This can make you more of a target for break-ins during the crisis. However, when you have a network of trusted friends in place before a crisis, you will all have much better odds of surviving it.

A neighborhood block party can be a good way to meet your neighbors.

RULE 12: GET YOUR HOME READY

One of the best case scenarios for surviving a crisis is to have a well-stocked, secure home. This allows you to shelter in place until the crisis is over. But no matter how well prepared your home is, some crises will force you to evacuate anyway. Other events will make it is safer to shelter in your home. When that happens, you will want it to be prepared. This way, survival will be more likely. And it will be as comfortable as possible. Of course, you'll need food, water, and first aid supplies. But there's more you can do to prepare your home for a crisis.

POWER

Power is everything in the modern home. Electricity helps us do virtually everything today. It heats our home and water. It helps us cook and keeps food from spoiling. It lights our home. It pumps water into the home. Electricity washes and dries our clothes and dishes. And it runs nearly all of our appliances.

ALTERNATIVES TO ELECTRICITY

The power grid is not always reliable even when there isn't a crisis. And it is one of the first things to go during a crisis. If you develop a plan to survive without a power grid, you'll be more secure. Even when extreme weather or blackouts threaten your power supply, your house will be fine. Your options for maintaining power are having a non-electric backup or an alternative power supply.

Non-electric alternatives can replace many of your home systems. A wood stove can heat your home. You can also use it to cook food and boil your water. The majority of basic electric appliances have manual alternatives. The more of them you have, the easier it will be to maintain your standard of living during a power outage.

SOLAR POWER

Solar power is the best way to equip your house so that you never lose electricity. Even in a blackout, you'll be fine. Solar arrays are becoming less expensive as the technology continues to develop. The average home can run on an array that costs less than $10,000. Spending several thousand dollars can seem like a large up-front commitment. But the system will pay for itself after four or five years. And it will be very useful if the power grid fails.

GENERATORS

Generators are good short-term solutions to power outages. But because they require a fuel source to work, they are not a sustainable option. In the event of a crisis, fuel will very quickly become scarce. You should not rely on anything that needs fuel for long-term survival. Generators also cannot be used indoors. They spew dangerous amounts of carbon monoxide.

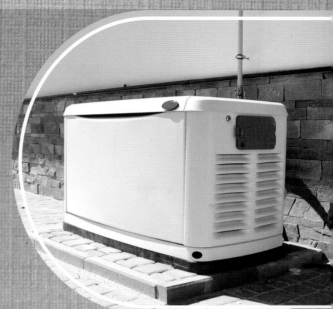

LIGHT

Lighting is the first thing to go in a power outage. There are several choices for other light sources. Long-life candles are small glass containers that are filled with liquid paraffin. They burn more brightly than wax candles. They also last much longer. Hurricane lamps should be in every survivalist's supply store. They have an adjustable wick. This lets you to increase or decrease the brightness and rate of fuel use. Hand-cranked flashlights are also an excellent investment. They don't need fuel or batteries to work.

HEAT

Heating is critical to survival. Even in a well-insulated house, when it's cold outside the temperature indoors can drop quickly if the furnace goes out. Hire a professional to perform an energy audit on your home. Utility companies do this for free. They will tell you where you are losing energy. Tightly insulate your home. And make it as energy efficient as possible.

WOOD STOVES

Make sure you also have a non-electric heating source. You also need plenty of fuel for it. A wood stove is an excellent asset. It can heat your entire home and cook your food. You will need to keep a rather large woodpile. Or, scout areas where you can collect wood. Make sure you know how to operate your wood stove before a crisis happens.

SECURE YOUR HOME

Home security is very important in a crisis. As supplies run low, looters and scavengers will grow increasingly desperate. They may eventually attempt to burglarize your home. The best deterrent is to make your home as difficult as possible to enter. You should already have security measures in place. This includes a home security system and double locks on doors and windows. Be prepared to further secure entry points to your home. Push heavy furniture against doors and windows. Or secure them with plywood and 2x4s. Own the right weapons to defend your home against intruders. And have an escape route in place if the house is breached. Making your house harder to get into than others in your area will make looters move on to easier targets.

A SIMPLE ILLUSION

One way to protect your home is to make it look like there's no reason to enter. This is true if large groups of looters are in your area. You want them to think it's empty. You can do this by making it look like its already been hit. This can be done without making it less secure. Make the front door looks like it's been kicked in or removed. This will make people will think the house is empty. Secure the front hall instead. This way, if intruders do enter, they won't be able to get too far. Keep windows boarded up and secure. Push heavy furniture against other entrances. The goal is to draw attention to the front door. If it looks like the only way in, good. Then all you have to do is make it look like someone's already entered and looted the house. If you use lights, even candles, only do it in rooms with blacked-out windows. The easiest way to tell if a house is occupied is if there is light coming from it. If you have to use loud machines like a generator, do it in the basement, and do so rarely. This will make it harder to pinpoint its location.

RULE 13: PREPARE TO IMPROVISE

It doesn't matter how well stocked you are. Sooner or later your supplies will start to dwindle. You won't be able to go to the local pharmacy to replace medical supplies. And you certainly won't be able to go shopping at the grocery. So what can you do?

PLAN AHEAD

The best way to ensure your food supplies do not run short is to produce and forage them yourself. On a standard city lot you can produce enough fruits and vegetables to feed a family of four. It will require a lot of planning and a lot of work. But it can be done. And you can also forage water supplies.

Let's say you have a garden and a means of collecting and purifying water. And you have supplies necessary to survive a long-term crisis. Chances are you are better equipped than many of the people in your area. That means that you can use your supplies, fresh vegetables, and potable water to barter with. This is especially true if you and your neighbors trust one another to work together to survive. Your fellow community gardeners may want to trade food or medical supplies for water or work. If you have skills, you will be a valuable asset to the community. Your neighbors will want to trade supplies for services.

Medical supplies can be valuable commodities in crisis situations.

BE CAUTIOUS

When you go out to scavenge, try to think like a homeless person. The homeless are masters of surviving on city streets. They know where to look for shelter and how to find food. The survival skills they use apply to an urban crisis. Think about where you see homeless people sleeping. Often you don't. That's because they hide themselves within the existing structures of the city. They find shelter under bridges and abandoned houses. They find spots that are tucked away. Why do they choose these spots? It's for their own safety. They know that if they are not seen, they are safer. Blend in with your surroundings in the same way. Alleys and gangways are excellent routes you can take without being seen. Always move together, and protect your rear and flanks from sudden attacks. Move quickly and quietly and stay out of sight.

A HIDDEN TRICK

The homeless also know one very important thing about scavenging. They understand that one person's trash is another's treasure. The homeless know how to find value in items others are throwing away. Keep that in mind when you are looking for supplies or food. Where are good spots to look? At the beginning of the crisis, search dumpsters. You may find non-perishables in grocery store dumpsters. There may be supplies in other retail stores' dumpsters. Looters will ransack the stores. But they will usually leave dumpsters alone. This is a great place to look for supplies.

HOMES AROUND YOU

Abandoned homes in your area are good places to look for supplies. Make absolutely certain that there is no one home before you break in. You don't want to enter a home in which a frightened and armed person is hiding. Take only what you need. Reseal the home behind you. This keeps it from becoming a target for squatters.

KEEP THINGS WORKING

Repair supplies and appliances as soon as they break. Learn how to keep them in good working order. Many items can be creatively improvised. Experiment with ways to do this before the crisis. You'll develop a familiarity with improvisation. That will help you when you are attempting to solve problems under pressure.

RULE 14: PLAN FOR THE LONG TERM

Whatever the crisis is, you should be ready to survive it for the long term. The residents of New Orleans who stayed during Hurricane Katrina assumed it would be a short-term crisis. They didn't think it would be different from the many hurricanes they had already weathered at home. They had no way of knowing that the storm surge would be one of the most powerful in history. They couldn't predict that the levees would break. They never expected the massive flooding. Few thought the civil authorities would unable to help. In any crisis, the situation is very unpredictable. It can always escalate from a short-term, low intensity situation into a long-term, high intensity one. When it does, there's usually very little warning.

BE READY

Thinking in terms of long-term survival is key. So is planning accordingly. This will ensure that your family is ready for anything. A 72-hour go bag and enough supplies to survive a week is a good start. But you also need to plan for a much longer crisis. By stocking enough supplies to last months, you can survive a long-term crisis. Your approach will be the same as with a short-term one. Having networks with members of your community, and plans for protecting your neighborhood is key. So is being self-reliant. If you are, you won't have much trouble adjusting to a crisis.

Don't be caught unawares in a crisis.

BE CONFIDENT

If you're confident about your long-term abilities, you'll also be much better prepared to deal with the initial crisis. There is peace of mind that comes with being completely prepared to shelter at home. This will let you to react to the crisis much more calmly. You'll make correct decisions and avoid putting yourself or your family in danger. You'll be able to decide whether to evacuate for solid reasons. You'll base your decision on the safety of your home. You won't need to worry whether your supplies will last if you stay put.

BE SELF-RELIANT

You may face a crisis that will have unknown duration or outcomes. This could be a government or economic collapse. When that happens, you want your home to be as self-reliant as possible. This will make you much better prepared to plan for the long-term. That's because you will not have to change much about your everyday routine. If you already have solar panels providing the power you need, outages are no problem. With a vegetable garden and a few chickens, you are growing your own food. Rainwater collection barrels and filtration solves the problem of water. And a compost bin provides you with waste disposal. With a wood-burning stove, you don't need to worry about heating. And with several months' worth of supplies, you're prepared for anything.

RULE 15: LIVE PREPARED

The key to surviving a crisis is proper preparation. You must avoid being one of the unlucky many who are forced to scramble for supplies at overwhelmed grocery stores. You don't want to be trapped inside without drinkable water, food, or medical supplies. And you don't want to be stuck in a traffic jam trying to escape the crisis. You want to be one of the prepared few who can weather the crisis.

THE IDEAL RESPONSE

This is the scenario that you want to prepare for. Safe in your secured, well-stocked home, you gather around the radio with your family. You receive reports and updates about the crisis as it develops. Perhaps you have an alternative power supply such as a solar array. Then you'll be able to watch TV news reports to get a clear picture of how the crisis will affect your family. You'll know whether you need to evacuate or if you will be safe in your home.

ADAPT YOUR LIFESTYLE

As the days go by, your daily habits won't change much from your regular routine. You'll continue to eat the kind of healthful meals you're used to. You'll have fresh or preserved vegetables from your garden. If you keep chickens, you'll have fresh eggs. Your water filtration system will ensure that you don't have to start using your emergency water supplies for a long time. If someone in your family is injured, you'll be prepared to stabilize them thanks to your first responder training. And you'll have all the supplies you need in your first aid kit to help them recover.

AT CRISIS END

Eventually, the situation will normalize. Your city or town will get back to normal. Or, the crisis will be so extreme that that it will become long term. But you will adapt to your new way of life. Since you were prepared, this won't be too much of an adjustment for you. You can work with your neighbors to secure your neighborhood from looters and share tips and supplies. You'll survive together thanks to the preparations you made before the crisis became truly real.

THE ULTIMATE GOAL

That is the goal of urban survival. You will be so prepared for any crisis that you will be able to survive. Survival means quickly and safely escaping the city before the crisis spins completely out of control. Or it may mean sheltering inside until the situation stabilizes. But the best chance you have of surviving it is being completely prepared.

CHAPTER 2:

BUILD YOUR RESOURCES & SKILLS

MAKE YOUR OWN CALORIE BAR

A great way to maintain your energy on a long hike or while you're out hunting is to carry calorie bars with you. These bars pack a ton of protein and energy into a small, light package. This means quite a few can fit into your backpack—enough for several days. Calorie bars also last for a very long time, which makes them the perfect addition to your home emergency stores or your go bags. If you have a bunch of calorie bars, you'll be able to survive for a while without worrying about where your next meal is going to come from. You can make calorie bars now and store them until you need them. You'll need to store your calorie bars in an airtight container and check them periodically to make sure they don't spoil. But if you make them correctly, that shouldn't be a problem.

WHY MAKE YOUR OWN?

Store-bought calorie bars are an option, of course. But they're expensive, especially when compared to the cost of making your own. You can also adjust the recipe provided here to make calorie bars that fit your personal tastes, which is not an option with store-bought calorie bars. This can be more important than you might think. If you have to rely on calorie bars in a survival situation for several weeks, you are going to want to make sure you like the way they taste!

RECIPE 1: FRUIT CALORIE BARS

Ingredients

- 2 cups oats
- 2½ cups powdered milk
- 1 cup sugar
- one (1) 3 oz. package fruit-flavored Jell-O
- 3 tablespoons water
- 3 tablespoons honey

1. Mix well the oats, powdered milk, and sugar in a large bowl.

2. In a medium saucepan, mix the Jell-O mix, water, and honey, and bring to a rolling boil. Boil until Jell-O is thoroughly dissolved. Remove from heat and allow to cool slightly.

3. Add the Jell-O mixture to the dry ingredients and mix thoroughly using a stand mixer or handheld electric mixer. If the consistency becomes too dry, add a bit of water one teaspoon at a time. Dough should not be wet, but it should stick together when pressed with your finger.

4. Line a 9"x13"baking pan with parchment paper. Press dough evenly and firmly into the pan.

5. Cut the dough into even, rectangular shaped bars. Be sure to cut all the way through the bars to prevent crumbling after you dry them. A pizza cutter will work best.

6. Bake at 200 degrees for 1.5–2 hours. Make sure the bars dry out completely, and while you cannot easily overcook them, check regularly after 1.5 hours. Cool on a wire rack.

7. Store bars in an airtight container until you are ready to use them. For camping trips, pack them individually by wrapping in plastic wrap.

RECIPE 2: CHOCOLATE CALORIE BARS

Ingredients

- 1 scoop chocolate protein powder
- 1 tbsp. cocoa powder
- ⅓ cup Splenda
- 1 cup oats
- 4 egg whites
- ½ cup unsweetened applesauce
- ¼ tsp vanilla extract
- 1 tbsp natural peanut butter

1. Preheat the oven to 350 degrees.

2. Mix the egg whites and uncooked oatmeal in a large bowl. Add the remaining ingredients.

3. Spray a nonstick cooking spray in an 8"x8" baking dish. Spread the mixture in an even layer, over the bottom of the dish. Cut into bars as described in Recipe 1.

4. Bake for about 15-20 minutes, or until the edge starts to pull away from the sides of the dish.

5. Cool on a wire rack and store in an airtight container.

These recipes will make about two dozen tasty calorie bars. These bars stay chewy even though they don't contain any moisture, which is important to prevent spoilage. They don't crumble easily and are compact enough that you can pack a lot of them in your backpack. They're the perfect thing to take on a hike or a hunting trip, and in a survival situation they're invaluable.

PACK YOUR 72-HOUR KIT

The 72-hour kit can be the difference between making it out of a survival scenario alive or not. One of the most overlooked components of a 72-hour kit, or go bag, is proper clothing. These are at least as important as the other supplies and tools you will have in your go bag. Often, having the right clothing is the most important consideration when you're trying to survive an emergency like a natural disaster or a collapse of civil order.

A RANGE OF SCENARIOS

The scary thing about survival situations is that you often have no warning before you're in one. Natural disasters can and do strike without warning, and in a collapse of civil authority, conditions can deteriorate very rapidly. You might be on vacation or on your way home from work when suddenly everything changes and now you have to fight to survive. When that happens, you won't want to have just your swim trunks or office wear to get through the situation. But without the right clothing in your go bag, that's precisely the kind of circumstances you can find yourself grappling with.

Outer layer
- Jacket
- Pants

Mid layer
- Fleece jacket
- Shirt

Base layer
- Thermal pants
- Thermal top
- Socks

BREATHABLE

WIND & RAIN

OUTER LAYER
WATERPROOF JACKET

MID LAYER
FLEECE

BASE LAYER
THERMAL PANTS & TOP

BODY HEAT

ADAPTABILITY

An important question when you're considering what clothes to keep in your go bag is whether or not you should pack for the current season. Some survivalists prefer this method, and switch out warm winter clothes for lighter summer gear as the seasons change. But this isn't always the best plan. When an emergency situation is unfolding—especially if it's a natural disaster—weather can change from mild to extreme in hours. And in a collapse of civil order, you may find that the survival scenario lasts for much longer than the 72 hours your bag is designed to support. For these reasons, it's best to carry a little extra weight and make sure you have clothing that will protect you no matter the weather. Of course, if you live in a Southern state, you probably won't need Arctic-grade snow gear, for example. But you will want a coat that will keep you warm if you have to flee your area and head north. Pack clothes that are adaptable to a variety of weather conditions.

DURABLE CLOTHING

Survival clothing should be selected for different attributes than normal clothing. You want clothes that will help protect you from a variety of threats when the situation is deteriorating quickly. For starters, your go-bag clothing should be tough and durable. It's going to be the only clothing you have for an unknown period of time. If you choose cheap material or poorly tailored clothes, they won't last. Your go-bag clothes should be comfortable, too. You may have to travel for days or even weeks, possibly on foot. In this scenario, you don't want to be wearing clothing that is too tight or chafes your skin—these seemingly minor annoyances can quickly turn into life-threatening injuries if you're not careful. Make sure your clothing is versatile and can adapt to all kinds of terrain, weather conditions, and emergency situations. It should be adaptable to running, climbing, and even swimming. It should dry quickly and be fairly simple to clean and maintain.

BLENDING IN

Your survival clothes should also be inconspicuous. Don't wear obvious camouflage gear, bright colors, or expensive, name-brand clothing. These all attract attention in densely populated areas. Muted, natural colors are best. These will help you blend in to a variety of background without alerting anyone to your presence. Finally, you should choose clothing made of natural fibers. That means cotton, denim, wool, and silk. Don't select poly-synthetic blends. They're more flammable, which can be very dangerous.

WHAT TO PACK

This list describes what you should have in a generalized go bag. Of course, you can and should adapt this list to suit the region you live in and the type of weather you typically expect across all seasons. Remember: you want muted, natural colors and natural fibers for all of your clothing.

- **Head Gear:** watch cap, baseball hat, and cowl or balaclava

- **Tops:** 2 cotton t-shirts, 2 cotton long-sleeved shirts, rain jacket or poncho, wool sweater and topcoat (depending on region). You'll want layers, so pack multiple shirts of varying thickness, as well as long underwear.

- **Bottoms:** Silk base layer, 2 pairs of pants—BDU with extra pockets is best, but avoid camo patterns. Durable denim jeans or work pants (such as Carharts) are also good for colder climates.

- **Footwear:** Multiple pairs of socks—at minimum eight pairs. Regularly changing your socks helps prevent trench foot. This is a bacterial infection of the feet caused by damp, dirty conditions. It can be painful and very dangerous in a survival situation. In colder regions, you will need wool socks. You should have one pair of hiking boots and another pair of running shoes. Strap-on sandals are also useful for hotter environments.

Accessories: Leather work gloves are your best bet. For your belt, get a "rigger's belt." These are extra-long and can serve as an improvised rope or tourniquet if you need one.

CHOOSE FIRE STARTERS

Fire is one of the most important tools for successfully homesteading or surviving a long-term breakdown of society. Along with finding or making shelter, getting clean water, and finding food, fire is right at the top. Fire is what allowed humans to move beyond the wilderness and begin surviving in a sustainable manner. Without fire, you won't be able to accomplish much in terms of homesteading or survival.

FIRE STARTING KIT

Because the ability to dependably start a fire is so vital to survival, you will need a fire starting kit that will last for a very long time. That means two things: One, you will be able to easily maintain it for many years, and two, it isn't a depletable resource that will eventually run out. Of course, you can have a massive cache of butane lighters or strike-anywhere matches, and these could last for a few years. But if you are looking for something you can depend on for an indefinite length of time, consider one of the following options.

MAGNESIUM FIRE STARTER

This device is similar to the traditional idea of flint. It's easy to use and very portable. All it requires is to scrape some magnesium shavings from the block using a blade, and then scraping the attached sparking mechanism next to the shavings quickly. A spark will quickly ignite the magnesium. These devices work whether they're dry or wet and produce a flame that's powerful enough to get kindling burning right away, whether it's damp or dry. The magnesium block itself is fire-resistant, so it's also very safe. And because you have everything you need to start a fire in the block, you won't have to worry about having enough fuel to get a fire going.

FERRO ROD

A Ferro Rod is a flint bar made of ferrocerium, which immediately creates superheated sparks that will start a fire whenever it's required. The product is small and lightweight, so it won't take up too much room in your go bag. The device requires two hands to operate, which has some drawbacks.

UST BLASTMATCH FIRE STARTER

This patented tool directs a jet of superheated sparks and produces more than twice the heat of a match. That allows the BlastMatch to ignite just about any flammable material very rapidly. You can also direct the superheated stream at various areas of the campfire to get it burning quickly, regardless of the weather conditions. If the device is damp, you can simply wipe it down and it will work just the same. It is guaranteed to work for the first thousand uses. The BlastMatch's spring-loaded system makes it compact, and its flint bar can be rotated 360 degrees. It's also very safe, with a safety catch that prevents accidental use.

UST SPARKIE FIRE STARTER

This device is made by Ultimate Survival Technologies, the same company that makes the BlastMatch. The Sparkie is designed to only require one hand to use, which helps you start a fire even in extreme weather conditions. It's also very compact and lighter than the BlastMatch. The Sparkie's flint mechanism can also be rotated 360 degrees, which helps prevent uneven wear. It has a rubber grip to improve control, and it's very simple to use.

UST WETFIRE STARTING TINDER

This product is an excellent complement to whatever fire starting device you have. The WetFire tinder will get a roaring fire going even in the worst conditions, and it will start a fire even in the middle of a rainstorm. It actually burns longer when it's wet. Each block of tinder is separately packaged, which prevents it from leaking into your other survival gear. They're smokeless and non-toxic, and don't come with the problems typically associated with petroleum fire starters. WetFire works at high altitudes, inclement weather and even in high winds.

While you should know how to gather and use natural tinder, a product such as WetFire tinder can make your job easier.

MAKE YOUR OWN PEPPER SPRAY

In a survival situation or following a collapse of civil order, self-defense and personal protection become persistent concerns. In addition to knowing how to defend yourself in hand-to-hand combat, it's a good idea to have tools to defend yourself and your home with. An outstanding nonlethal close-range weapon is pepper spray. It allows you to quickly put an attacker down long enough to escape a life-threatening situation.

WHY MAKE YOUR OWN?

Pepper spray, bear spray, and other chemical irritant weapons can be purchased legally. But in a post-collapse situation, you may not be able to find them as readily. But that doesn't mean you can't make your own. You can get almost all of the ingredients for pepper spray from your garden and home, which means they should remain fairly available even after a collapse of civil order or a natural disaster. Simple pepper spray requires two things: dried hot peppers with a high Scoville rating and a medium to carry the pepper oil to the attacker's vulnerable areas. If you stock up on these materials now, you'll be prepared to make your own pepper spray after a collapse.

CHILI PEPPERS

Dried chili peppers are the primary ingredient of pepper spray. The chemical that gives chili peppers their "heat" is called capsaicin. This chemical is what makes food spicy, and it's what gives pepper spray the ability to induce pain and temporary blindness. The more capsaicin a pepper contains, the better it will be in pepper spray.

THE SCOVILLE UNIT

The Scoville Unit is the scale on which the "heat" of chili peppers is measured. The pepper sprays used by law enforcement agencies in the United States typically have a Scoville rating between 500,000 and 5 million Scoville Units. At minimum, you will want to use chili peppers that have a Scoville rating of 200,000 or higher. While each individual pepper will have its own level of Scoville Units, this handy guide will give you an idea of the range certain peppers are in:

• Bird's eye chili peppers have a Scoville rating from 100,000–225,000 SU.

• Habañero chili peppers have a Scoville rating from 100,000–350,000 SU.

• Red Savina habañero peppers have a Scoville rating from 350,000–580,000 SU.

• Bhut Jolokia (Ghost) peppers have a Scoville rating from 850,000–1.04 million SU

SCOVILLE SCALE

CAROLINA REAPER
(1,400 000 - 2,200 000)
TRINIDAD SCORPION (1,200 000 - 2,000 000)
GHOST (855 000 - 1,041 427)
CHOCOLATE HABANERO (425 000 - 577 000)
RED SAVINA HABANERO (350 000 - 577 000)
FATALI (125 000 - 325 000)
HABANERO (100 000 - 350 000)
SCOTCH BONNET (100 000 - 350 000)
THAI (50 000 - 100 000)
PEQUIN (40 000 - 58 000)
CAYENNE (30 000 - 50 000)
AJI (30 000 - 50 000)
TABASCO (30 000 - 50 000)
ARBOL (15 000 - 30 000)
SERRANO (10 000 - 23 000)
HUNGARIAN (5 000 - 10 000)
CHIPOTLE (5 000 - 8 000)
JALAPENO (2 500 - 8 000)
POBLANO (1 000 - 1 500)
ANAHEIM (500 - 2 500)
PEPPERONCINI (100 - 500)
BELL PEPPER (0)

PEPPER SPRAY RECIPE

Ingredients and Supplies

• 6–12 chili peppers, preferably selected from the guide above. The more peppers you use, the higher the amount of capsaicin and the more effective your pepper spray will be.

• 2 tbsp. minced garlic

• 2 cups vinegar or isopropyl rubbing alcohol. This will be the carrier that delivers the pepper spray's punch to the attacker.

• 2 tbsp. mineral oil. This causes the spray to adhere to the target.

• Latex or rubber gloves

• Eye protection

• Mask for nose and mouth protection. The best mask for this job is an N95 respirator. If you don't have one, you can soak a bandanna in lemon juice and tie it snugly over your nose and mouth.

• Knife and cutting board

• Sealable jar or bottle

• Cheesecloth

• Funnel

METHOD

• Completely dry the chili peppers by hanging them in a well-ventilated area for a few weeks. You can also use a dehydrator to dry them out, or heat them in an oven set to 130–150 degrees Fahrenheit.

• Remove the stems and finely mince the peppers. You must be careful not to lose the oils and juice of the peppers while you're cutting them. A food processor works great for mincing the peppers while retaining the oils.

• Mince or process the garlic.

• Combine all ingredients in a food processor, blender, or mixing bowl. Once you have a consistent mix, push it through a sieve to strain out any large pieces of organic matter.

• Leave in a cool place (preferably a refrigerator) for 24–48 hours to allow the ingredients to combine.

• Spread the cheesecloth across the base of the funnel mouth, and slowly pour the mixture into the jar or bottle. Remove excess chunks as they build up on the cheesecloth and discard.

Storage and Use

This recipe should give you about ten ounces of pepper spray. Keep it in a cool place (preferably a refrigerator or icebox) in a sealed container. It should remain viable for up to 2–3 months. A simple spray bottle works as a delivery mechanism. It's important to find one that has a range of about ten feet with a fairly concentrated stream. Don't use spray bottles that produce a fine mist when you spray them; these can result in the pepper spray blowing back into your own face.

DIY SOLAR-POWERED CELL PHONE CHARGER

In the current era, devices powered by USB connections are abundant. Many of these devices are essential parts of every person's daily communication and access to information. If you are hiking in a remote area, on a long car trip, or camping, you'll need a plan to keep your devices working. Whether it's your laptop, smartphone, speakers, or other devices, you can use a portable solar cell phone charger to make sure it doesn't run out of juice. This isn't just for convenience, either. It can also impact your ability to call for first responder help in an emergency.

CONVENIENCE AND SECURITY

Furthermore, even if you're safe at home, what happens if the power goes out? You'll need to have an alternate to make sure your devices keep working so you can maintain communication with family members and close friends. This becomes especially critical when the power failure has been the result of an extreme weather event, civil unrest, or a natural disaster. In these kinds of situations, you'll have to be prepared to keep your USB-powered devices working—often for a prolonged period of time. Doing so means you'll be able to keep tabs on the situation as it develops, maintain communications with the outside world, and avoid more life-threatening emergencies.

This hiker uses a solar panel to charge her laptop.

MAKE YOUR OWN

You can construct a reliable, functional, and portable USB solar charger at an affordable cost and with very basic techniques. When you combine a solar charger with a USB power bank, which is basically a big rechargeable battery, you can continue charging your devices after the sun goes down. USB power banks can be completely charged in less than two hours. They also have clearly understandable battery power indicators so you'll know your power status at all times.

Components of a USB Solar Charger Include:

• Water Proof & Shock Resistant 10-volt, 3-watt Solar Panel

• 2800mAh Power Bank with AA outlet and iPhone compatibility

• Self-contained and reliable

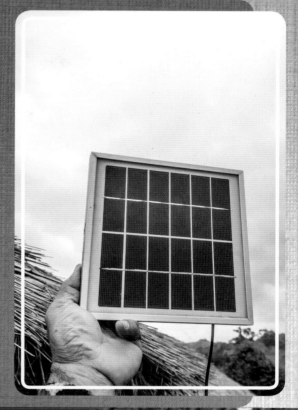

SUGGESTIONS

It's best to use a solar panel that has been rated to between 3–10 watts and 6–10 volts. This will ensure that you can quickly charge your device or USB power bank. The materials required for the charger can be obtained online or at a local hardware store for 20 dollars or less, although finding the best prices may take some sleuthing. Power banks are also very affordable. A high-quality model should be available for $20 or less.

MATERIALS:

- 10 Volt, 3Watt, 400mAh Solar Panel
- USB Power Bank–2800 mAh with battery indicator
- 4-port USB hub
- 7805 regulator chip
- Micro USB cable with stripped end
- Leatherman or other multitool
- 12" stranded wire
- Superglue

CONSTRUCTION

The 7805 Regulator

The recommended solar panel produces about 10 volts over 3 watts, and the power bank has a 5-volt capacity. The voltage discrepancy means a regulator is necessary to keep the power bank from being overcharged and burning out. Fortunately, a regulator is fairly simple to build.

1. Solder the micro-USB plug into the regulator.
2. Solder two wires to the regulator. They will connect to the positive and negative leads on the solar panel.
3. Attach the regulator to the terminal block of the solar panel with superglue.
4. Trim the heat sink mount from the regulator using the multitool.
5. Solder the regulator wires to the solar panel. Make sure you're attaching positive to positive, and negative to negative!

Once you have completed these steps, you're all set. You can directly power your USB-powered devices from the solar charger. A power bank isn't required for charging, but they are inexpensive and useful enough that you'd be remiss to not have at least one on hand.

MOUNTING USB DEVICES

Hopefully, you'll choose to get a power bank and a USB hub. If you do, it's helpful to mount them on the back of the solar charger. This makes them easier to use and ensures you won't lose them. You can attach them to the solar charger using a hot glue gun or epoxy. These have the advantage of being safe and easy to use, and they'll keep the devices from coming lose if the charger is bumped or dropped.

Mount the power bank with the adhesive. Then, connect the charging cable from the solar panel to the charge input on the power ban. Finally, plug the USB hub into the output on the power bank.

Now you're all set. You can start using the solar-powered array as soon as the glue dries! With the proper care and maintenance, the solar panel should last for many years. The completed array should be small enough to easily fit in your car's glove compartment or in your go-bag. It's light enough that if you keep it in your backpack while hiking or camping, you'll barely even notice it's there.

OPERATE A HAM RADIO

For decades, HAM radio has been popular among hobbyists. Before the advent of the internet, HAM radio was one of the best ways to connect with other people around the globe. It's also a very useful tool to know how to use in a survival situation. Following a natural disaster or collapse of civil society, it's unlikely that cell phones or internet will be functioning, and even landline connections could be down. But HAM radios don't rely on existing infrastructure to send their messages out to the world. They're a great alternative communications tool that can keep you in touch with your family or your survivor network following an emergency.

GETTING YOUR TICKET

Licenses are required to operate a HAM radio. The good news is, they aren't very expensive or difficult to obtain. All you need to do is pay a small fee and take a simple exam about radio use. This is called "Getting your ticket" by HAM operators. The Amateur Radio Relay League is a great resource to help prepare you for your exam and find a testing site nearby. Depending on how far you want to legally broadcast, you can test into various levels of operator rights:

• Technician: this level operator is permitted to transmit up to 100 watts on a limited number of frequencies.

• General: this level operator is permitted to transmit up to 1500 watts and operate on a larger number of frequencies

• Extra: this level operator is permitted to transmit up to 1500 watts on all frequencies.

Of course, after a collapse of civil order, the license level won't be an issue. In the meantime, though, it's a good idea to get some practice on a General level. This will give you a solid understanding of how the radio operates and give you a good idea of the range you can obtain at 1500 watts.

TRANSCEIVERS

A HAM radio operator needs a few items to get started, once they've gotten their license and are ready to go. The transceiver is a combination transmitter/receiver. The price range on transceivers is fairly broad. Higher wattage transceivers are more expensive. Of course, in a survival situation you will probably want to be able to broadcast as far and as wide as possible to reach whatever help is out there. For most scenarios, however, something in a $200 to $500 range is usually appropriate.

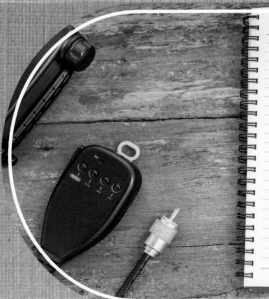

POWER SUPPLY

You'll also need a power supply for your transceiver. This can be pretty simple and usually falls under $100 in price. You will need to ensure the power supply is compatible with the transceiver you have. You want to give it enough power to operate reliably, but not so much that you're in danger of blowing a fuse or frying your electronics.

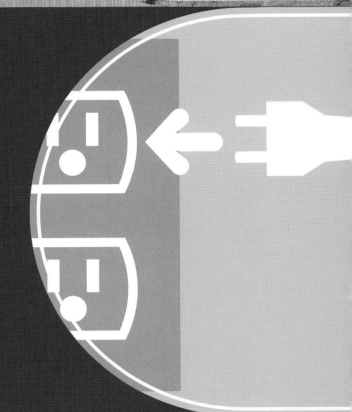

ANTENNA

The antenna is what lets you send outgoing and receive incoming messages. You can get an antenna that can pick up frequencies from very far away for about $100. You may have to consider local zoning laws and see what they have to say about mounting the antenna; not all areas allow large antennas on residential structures.

TUNER

A manual or auto tuner lets you select the frequency you're broadcasting and receiving messages on. For novice HAM radio operators, auto tuners are usually best. The tuner will link the transceiver to the antenna, so you have to make sure it is compatible with both pieces of equipment.

The microphone is what lets you talk to other HAM radio operators. It's a good idea to also get a key for sending messages in Morse code. You don't need a very expensive microphone for HAM radio broadcasting, mid-range mics are just fine.

CABLES AND PARTS

Finally, you will need cables to connect all the components of your HAM radio. It's also a good idea to have extra cables, just in case anything happens to your operating cables. After a collapse, you may not be able to easily acquire this kind of equipment. The same is true for other replaceable parts such as fuses or wires. In a survival scenario, you won't be able to take the radio to your local electronics shop—you'll have to repair it on your own.

OPERATION

To operate the HAM radio once you've got it assembled and working, turn it on and use the tuner to get it to match the tuner as close to 1-to-1 as possible. Find an open frequency with the tuner, and you're ready to start broadcasting. It's a good rule of radio etiquette to check as whether a frequency is open before you start using it to broadcast. And in a survival scenario, you may want to tune into a frequency already in use and listen in before you send a message. You can also use Morse code to check for open frequencies by sending the letters Q, R, L.

RAIN GUTTER COLLECTION

Potable water—meaning water that is safe to cook with and drink—is one of the most difficult supplies to acquire in a survival situation. It's also one of the most critical items. Without water, you will die. There is no way around this fact. And unless you have a well, stream, or other natural supply of potable water on or near your homestead, you will need to store reserves of water. These can run out quickly, though. And they can also become contaminated by pollutants, poisons, or bacteria, all of which will render them undrinkable. Fortunately, rainwater can help refill your water stores very quickly, provided you know how to collect it.

Don't think of it as a rainy day, but as a way to collect resources.

BENEFITS OF RAIN GUTTERS

One of the best ways to collect rain water is with a rain gutter collection system. This will allow you to capture all of the runoff from your roof—and that amount can be considerable. And even before a collapse of civil order or other major emergency, collecting rainwater is a great way to reduce your water bills and make your homestead more self-sufficient and environmentally friendly.

CHECK THE REGULATIONS

A word of caution: In some states or municipalities, there are laws in place to prevent private individuals from collecting rainwater—even if they are on their own property. While the motives and impacts of these laws are questionable, prior to a collapse they are still in effect. Make sure you're familiar with any prohibitions against collecting rainwater and regulations that spell out how you can do it if it is legal.

MATERIALS

Here's what you'll need to construct a rain gutter water collection system:

- Paint strainer
- Five-gallon bucket
- 55-gallon drum with lid
- Downspout fittings
- Gutter strainer
- Three cinder blocks
- 3/4" spigot with 1/4" turn ball valve
- Permanent black marker
- Jigsaw
- Power drill with 7/8" spade bit
- Half-round bastard file
- Utility knife
- 1 1'4" galvanized wood screws

INSTRUCTIONS

Here are the steps you need to follow to make your rain gutter water collector:

1. Drill a starter hole eight inches from the top in the side of the 5-gallon bucket with the 7/8" spade bit. Use the jigsaw to cut around the bucket, leaving you with an eight-inch-tall ring.

2. Trace an outline of the top of the 5-gallon bucket on the top of the 55-gallon drum using the permanent marker.

3. Drill a hole in the top of the 55-gallon drum with the 7/8" spade bit. Following the outline you made with the permanent marker, use the jigsaw to cut out a circle. The top of the bucket should slide snugly into the opening on top of the drum.

4. Use the 7/8" spade bit to drill a hole on the side of the drum near the bottom. File the inside of the hole down using the half-round bastard file.

5. Screw the ¾" spigot securely into the hole. If you are having trouble getting it to fit securely, file the hole down a bit more.

6. Place the three cinder blocks upright and next to one another at the side of the house. Place the drum on top of the blocks, making sure it sits securely and is not in danger of falling.

You'll have to extend the downspout of your rain gutter so it connects to your reservoir. Here's how to do it:

1. Extend the existing downspout on your gutter to run down to meet the rainwater reservoir.

2. Measure where you will need to cut the downspout so it will meet the top of the reservoir, and mark it with permanent marker.

3. Using a utility knife, cut the extension and fit it onto the existing downspout.

4. Secure it to the side of the house using fittings and brackets.

5. Trace the outline of the end of the downspout on the lid of the 5 gallon bucket. Use the 7/8" spade bit to drill a starter hole, and cut along the outline with the jigsaw.

6. Secure the downspout in the whole on the lid of the 5 gallon bucket.

A few final considerations:

1. To prevent mosquitoes from getting into your water reservoir, tie a knot in your paint strainer and secure it across the top of the bucket.

2. Secure the lid on the bucket, over the paint strainer.

3. Place a gutter strainer in the opening of the downspout at the gutter. This will prevent the downspout from being clogged by large debris.

BUILD YOUR OWN ROOT CELLAR

Cold-season crops like potatoes, turnips, and yams are very useful. One of the reasons for this is because they will keep for months when properly stored. They don't need much— just a cool, well-ventilated space is enough. A spare refrigerator is one option, but what happens if you lose power for an indefinite period of time?

OUTDOORS VS. INDOORS

A much better option is a root cellar. These have been used to store food staples for centuries. Root cellars are more spacious than refrigerators and are very useful for long-term vegetable storage. Usually, a root cellar was kept close to or even below the home. The ground insulated the root cellar, and by constructing ventilation they had enough air flow to maintain the right temperature even during the warmest summer months. During the winter, vents would be closed to keep the cellar from freezing.

VENTILATION

Modern insulation has made the average home's basement too warm to successfully store vegetables for the long term. But you can still build a root cellar in your basement without too much effort. The key is ventilation. By creating the right flow of cold air to maintain the root cellar's temperature, you can keep vegetables for a long time. You'll have to watch the outside temperature, of course, and like traditional root cellars, close the vents when the weather drops too far below freezing. Most vegetables are damaged to the point that they're no longer useful if they freeze improperly, so this is very important to keep in mind.

CHOOSE A PLACE

Regardless of where you live or what kind of basement you have, there are a few key concepts that will apply to your root cellar. The first has to do with where you place your root cellar. You'll need to keep it ventilated with fresh air. That means it should be positioned in an area of the basement that has a window. Of course, if your basement doesn't have windows you can cut a hole in the wall, but this can be extremely difficult and can damage the home's foundation. It's far more advisable to use existing windows. If your area has harsh winters, you can also insulate the ventilation around a window.

WINDOWS

To insulate window ventilation, cut a 1-inch thick piece of polystyrene insulating foam and two pieces of ½-inch exterior-grade plywood to fit the window. Attach the plywood on both sides of the foam with polyurethane adhesive.

If there's a window available near a corner of your basement, even better. The outer walls of the basement are ideal for maintaining the right temperatures for a root cellar. By putting the root cellar in the corner, you increase the ratio of its exterior walls to interior walls by a factor of two. It also means you won't need to construct as many interior walls. Lastly, if you can meet all of these requirements—exterior wall, in a corner, near a window—and do so on the north side of the building, then you have the perfect conditions for your root cellar.

INTERIOR WALLS

Next, you'll need to build the interior walls of your root cellar. Before you begin buying or cutting any wood for your walls, measure the space and draw up a plan on paper. The root cellar doesn't have to be very big. A space that is about six feet by six feet is usually more than adequate. After you determine what kind of footprint the root cellar should have, build a frame for the walls and doorway. The walls do not need to be load-bearing, which will simplify this project considerably. If you're on a tight budget, the studs can be as much as two feet apart from one another.

When you cut the wall studs, leave about a quarter inch between the top of the wall and the joists above them. That will allow you to set the wall in place and secure it to the floor and ceiling. Secure the wall with number 10, 3½-inch screws. Then use wood glue and a tapered, soft wood wedge to fill the gap between the ceiling and joists.

Basement floors can often be damp. Because of this it's preferable to use a composite decking material or treated wood for the bottom of the wall. A solid composite decking material can be installed just like a wooden wall plate. Depending on your plans, you can pre-drill holes in the floor of the basement, or use a construction adhesive and concrete nails. While you might want to install a wooden door, it's not the best option. A PVC-strip door like the kind seen in walk-in freezers is better. It's easier to install than a wooden door, will keep cold air in more effectively, and gives you some wiggle room on designing the doorway.

INSULATION

Stiff foam sheets make the best insulation, but you can also use fiberglass batts. Foam sheets will resist mold and water damage better, and these are constant worries in maintaining a root cellar. You may have to cover your insulation with fire-retardant material. If you're using extruded polystyrene—one of the best insulators—then fire retardant is practically a requirement. While designing insulation, make sure you don't forget to consider the ambient heat coming from the basement ceiling.

VENT

The last thing to optimize is your dual-ventilation system. If possible, locate the intake and exhaust pipes on opposite sides of the root cellar. The exhaust should be located near the ceiling and the intake should be lower. This will help maximize the airflow through the space. Cover the vent openings with wire screens at both ends to prevent vermin from getting in. To maximize vegetable exposure to the airflow, wire racks are best.

BUILD AN OUTDOOR MUD OVEN

Following a civil collapse or major natural disaster, you will need to have a reliable means of cooking good food. Developing this now is also a great way to make your existing homestead more self-sufficient and, in the long run, more sustainable. As short-term solutions, rocket stoves and campfires are great. But they can be expensive and difficult to maintain for many years. They also have very few options for baking. A far better alternative is a do-it-yourself mud oven. These hardy appliances are based on technology that dates back thousands of years, which has the added benefit of not requiring fossil fuels or other modern inventions to operate them.

AN ANCIENT TECHNOLOGY

You don't need much to build a mud oven. All it takes is a mixture of clay and sand that can be fired into a sturdy, effective structure that can keep heat inside and cook food slowly and evenly. Once you've built the mud oven, all it takes to cook with it is to build a campfire inside the oven. Allow the fire to burn down. In this time, it will produce enough heat for the oven to be at the right temperature to cook your meal. Mud ovens have many names. They have also been called Earth Ovens, Adobe Ovens, Beehive Ovens, and—in Latin America—*El Horno*.

You can use any kind of flammable material for your mud oven, from forest underbrush to broken-down wooden furniture. The design of the oven means you can get it heated up to nearly 500 degrees Fahrenheit without using a very big fire. The base and walls of the mud oven serve as an effective heat sink that will stay hot enough to bake bread and proteins like beans and chicken easily and quickly.

THREE SIMPLE SKILLS

There are three skills involved in constructing a Mud Oven. They are: making sun-dried mud bricks, making mud mortar, and plastering with mud. You'll also need to know how to work with adobe to sculpt a small domed roof. These skills were developed thousands of years before modern construction methods were invented. The methods are simple enough that you can use them without many resources. These criteria—ancient and simple—are what make a technique ideal for a post-collapse project.

SUN-DRIED MUD BRICK MAKING

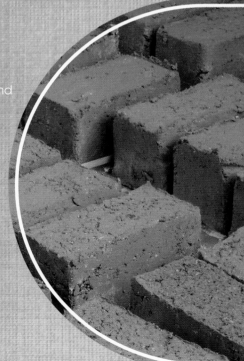

This is one of the oldest and simplest methods of construction. In making the oven, you will build the vault and dome with sun-dried mud bricks, and bond them together with mud mortar. In most locations, the material you need to build the oven are right beneath your feet. The proportion of sand to clay in mud bricks should be about 70% to 30%. Mix sand and clay into a slurry in this proportion, and form the bricks using a 4" x 8" x 2 ½" wooden cast or by hand.

Leave the bricks out in the hot summer sun and let them dry completely. Be on the lookout for cracks that develop while the bricks are drying. You'll have to discard any bricks that have more than three cracks, or cracks that are more than two inches long or 1/8 inch wide. Such cracks will result in an oven that is unstable and could collapse.

BUILD THE FOUNDATION

Some of the earliest known records of hand-built mud ovens date back to the Biblical city of Jericho. When you construct a mud oven by hand, you're able to make the walls thin enough to dry quickly and bond more efficiently to the mud mortar. The walls should be thick enough to retain heat, though! About 4–8 inches in thickness is perfect. Build the oven foundation in stages and let each layer completely dry before laying the next one on top of it. You'll have to elevate the foundation to keep the oven off the ground. This will help keep it dry and make it easier to use. You can set the foundation's height between one and three feet.

• Lay down a base of mud bricks in a circle about 3 feet wide, and fill in the center of the circle with a mud/clay slurry. Allow this to completely dry.

• Using mud mortar, build up the walls of the foundation to the desired height. Allow to completely dry.

• Fill in the foundation with mud slurry in successive layers, allowing each to dry. This foundation will hold the most heat when you are cooking with the oven.

• You can simply use the mud foundation—as the ancients did—or, if you have access to fire bricks, you can lay these on top of the foundation for your cooking floor.

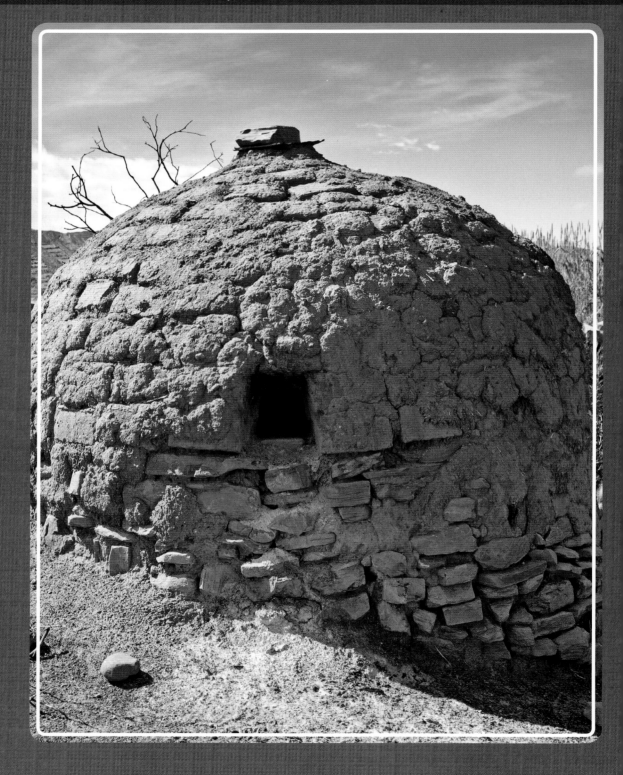

BUILD THE OVEN

There are a few ways to make the curved walls of the mud oven:

• Lay mud bricks flat and corbel them inward mortaring as you work. "Corbel" means jut the bricks inward. Or, incline each of the bricks at increasingly steep angles by adding more layers of mortar as you work up towards the ceiling of the oven, or...

• Use sand as a mold on top of which you will lay the mud slurry plaster.

Choose your method of construction based on the available materials and your personal preference. Do you prefer to make more mud bricks, or place multiple layers of mud slurry over the mold? Something to keep in mind: If you choose the slurry method, you'll have to cut an opening in the wall of the oven. With bricks, you can simply build it. But you'll have to layer mud plaster over the bricks if you choose that method.

You may want to leave a small opening at the top of the mud oven that serves as a smokestack. If you do so, you'll also need to make a chimney cover that will keep heat in the oven when you are cooking.

BEFORE USE

It's important to make sure the oven has dried completely before using it. It may take several days or even weeks, depending on the weather and available sunlight in your area. Your first fire should be small, so as to prevent the walls from cracking.

BUILD YOUR OWN FARADAY CAGE

A Faraday cage is a simple structure that blocks electromagnetic fields from entering or exiting it. The design, which is about 200 years old, guards objects inside the cage from high levels of static and non-static electricity. Faraday cages can accomplish this in a variety of ways: They can absorb incoming electromagnetic fields, reflect them, or create opposing fields that effectively cancel out incoming signals. They can protect sensitive electronic equipment from electromagnetic pulses (EMPs) like those that can be caused by nuclear weapons. And they can prevent anyone from accessing electronic hardware stored inside. Because of these reasons, it's a good idea to keep any radios, GPS devices, spare wireless phones, and laptops stored in a Faraday cage.

WHAT SHAPE?

A Faraday cage can be any shape you like—it can be a cylinder, a sphere, or a cube. Any enclosed space that has an outer layer that can conduct electricity will work as a Faraday cage. The cage's infrastructure can serve as the conductor. Or, you can build the cage out of materials that do not conduct electricity, such as wood, and then cover that with conductive material. For the conductor, you can use something as easy as multiple layers of aluminum foil. The simplicity of the cage means it is a relatively easy project that won't break your wallet.

HOW DOES IT WORK?

When an incoming electromagnetic field encounters the conductive material on the outside of the Faraday cage, the free electrons in the conductive material instantly realign themselves, blocking the incoming electricity. This only works if the cage or the material it's wrapped in are conductive. Otherwise, the free electrons won't be able to realign and the cage won't work.

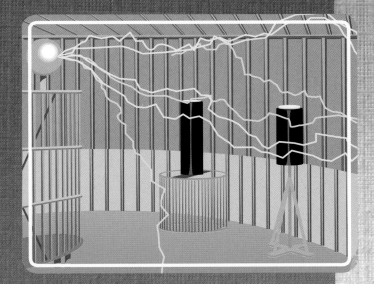

The layers of conductive material don't have to be very thick for the cage to do its job, though. Because of the "skin effect," which is the tendency of electrical currents to take a path along the outer layer of a conductor, a relatively thin surface will work for your cage. The skin effect is measured by a function of the incoming electromagnetic field wave and the type of material used in the conducting material. That function is called the "skin depth." If the layer of conductive material is larger than that depth—which is typically small—then the Faraday cage will have high levels of absorption loss. A cage with high absorption loss will be an excellent shield from incoming electromagnetic fields. And simply by wrapping the cage in five to ten layers of aluminum foil, you will achieve the necessary skin depth to protect your electronic equipment from even the kind of high-frequency electromagnetic fields generated by a nuclear bomb.

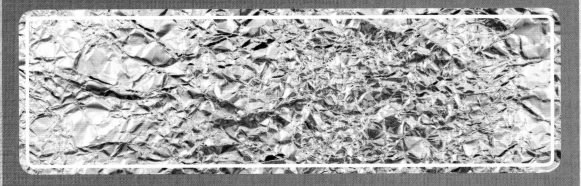

Michael Faraday, the inventor of the Faraday cage

CONDUCTIVE MATERIALS

The conductive material you choose will likely not have much effect on how well the cage protects your electronic equipment from high-frequency electromagnetic fields. Very conductive metals have a smaller skin depth. Silver, for example, has a skin depth of less than 5 microns at 200 megahertz. At that same frequency, the skin depth of aluminum is much higher—about 25 microns. But a micron is vanishingly small: a human hair is about 75 microns in diameter. With several sheets of heavy-duty aluminum foil, the conductive layer of the cage will be much deeper than the skin depth you'll need.

A Faraday cage can have small imperfections and even holes in it. Because electromagnetic fields travel in waves, any holes smaller than the wavelength of the incoming fields you wish to block will not matter. Because of this, you can build a cage out of fine aluminum mesh. You will still experience some loss via the door to the cage. This can be reduced significantly by insulating the seams around the door with tape made from conductive material.

CONTAINERS

It's not necessary to build a standalone Faraday cage, either. You can scavenge, barter, or buy a perfectly fine container that will double as a cage, such as a metal ammunition box, metal garbage cans, anti-static pouches, and even old microwave ovens. Different found objects will provide varying levels of effectiveness. No matter what you select, your main concern should be making sure you close gaps and seams to prevent electromagnetic leaks. While it's not necessary to ground the Faraday cage for it to work, you may wish to do so anyway. Grounding the cage will help prevent charge from building up in it, a situation that could be dangerous.

SHIELD ROOMS

You can also build a shield room in your house. These are rooms that are effectively Faraday cages, and they're often used in the tech industry to store sensitive electronics. To make one, cover the inside of a small room or closet with multiple layers of aluminum foil. Overlap the foil edges, and tape the seams with cellophane tape. Cover up all the outlets and light switches as well as the floor. Place a plywood board on the floor to walk on. Your shield room can store all of your emergency electronics and keep them safe from high-frequency electromagnetic fields.

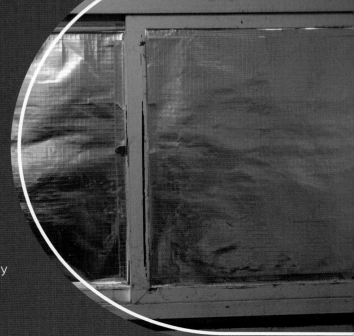

MAKE YOUR OWN CROSSBOW

A crossbow is an excellent piece of field equipment. It's particularly useful for when you want to hunt small game. Like a bow and arrow, its ammunition is reusable, and the weapon is virtually silent. It also has the ease of use of a rifle stock and trigger pull. These features combine to make a good crossbow one of the best survival tools you can have.

MATERIALS

You can buy a high-quality hunting crossbow to keep on hand as one of your primary go-bag weapons. And following a breakdown of civil order or a natural disaster, you may be able to loot one from a sporting goods store. This is risky and not recommended unless you know what you're doing, however. And what happens if neither of these options are available? You can build a simple, effective hunting crossbow from fairly basic, easy-to-scavenge parts. Here's what you'll need:

2 x pine two by fours, about 3 feet long

1x 1" PVC pipe, about 3 feet long

Nylon string

2 x miniature steel pulleys

6 x heavy-duty tie clips

2 x 2" wood screws

2 x 4" wood screws

1 x 2" wood nail

PVC or wood glue

¼" wood dowels

MAKE THE STOCK

1. Take a yard-long pine 2x4 and hold it against the shoulder of your dominant hand as you would a rifle stock. Find a comfortable length and mark the 2x4 at that length as well as where it feels most comfortable to place the trigger grip. Making the stock longer will increase the crossbow's power, but don't make it so long that you won't be able to use it comfortably. Saw off the end past the length mark. Draw a rectangle four inches long by one inch wide around the spot where you marked the trigger grip. Cut this rectangle out of the wood using a chisel, drill and rasp, and sand the edges.

2. Cut a 1/8 inch groove across the rectangular hole, towards the front of the hole. This will hold the crossbow string.

3. Cut a 1/4 inch channel down the exact middle of the top of the stock, starting from the rectangular hole and continuing to the end of the stock. Sand until it is smooth.

4. Cut a 22-inch piece of pine wood and attach it to the bottom of the stock using PVC glue. This will be the grip you will hold while firing the crossbow. If you like, you can shape it into a curved surface to make the grip more comfortable to hold.

MAKE THE BOW

5. With a hacksaw, cut a PVC pipe to 35.5 inches long. Cut a notch at each end that is wide enough to accommodate a small woodscrew. Insert screws at both ends. Use a 2-tie clip to attach a pulley to each woodscrew.

6. Cut a 1-inch deep groove in the front end of the stock that is wide enough to hold the PVC pipe. Using two wood screws, attach the PVC pipe to the front of the stock. The screws should be long enough to firmly hold the PVC pipe to the crossbow stock.

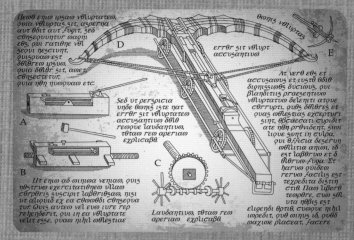

Crossbows are ancient weapons. This one was designed by da Vinci.

7. Tie the nylon string securely to the woodscrew on the left end of the PVC bow. Loop the string under the crossbow stock and through the pulley on the right side of the bow. Come back over the top of the crossbow stock and loop it through the pulley on the left. Bring the string back under the stock and tie it securely to the woodscrew on the right side of the bow. Only the firing string should be above the crossbow stock. Draw the firing string back and make sure it fits securely in the firing groove. The string should pull taut when it is placed in the firing groove.

A handmade crossbow

MAKE THE TRIGGER MECHANISM

8. Cut an L-shaped piece of wood that is 7/8 of an inch wide. It will need to fit snugly into the trigger housing but still be able to move more or less freely. Cut a 1/8-inch channel across the bottom of the L. Drill a hole through the angle of the L.

9. Place the L in the trigger housing with the groove up and the L pointing forward. Attach it to the crossbow stock by driving a nail through the stock housing and the hold at the angle of the L. The L should be placed so that it can "pop" the crossbow string out of the trigger groove when it is pulled.

MAKE THE BOLTS/ARROWS

10. Notch one end of each of the wooden dowels so they fit snugly onto the nylon string. Sharpen the other end to a very sharp point. You can harden the point of the dowel with fire. The bolts are lightweight, and you should be able to shoot them up to 50 yards.

THE KNIFE

A good knife is an essential survival tool. You should have one in your go bag or on your person in case of an emergency. A survival knife will literally make the difference between life and death in a number of survival scenarios. Without a knife it's very difficult to build shelter, dress wild game, or construct or repair survival tools.

BUY A KNIFE

You don't just want to grab a knife from the chopping block in your kitchen and stuff it in your go bag. To set yourself up for survival, you want to invest in a durable survival knife with a blade of about four to eight inches that can serve a variety of purposes. How can you choose from the many survival knives on the market?

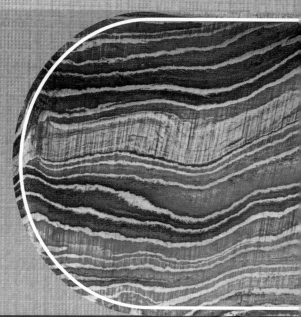

MATERIAL

In a long term survival situation, you want a knife that will last and that will sharpen easily. Many experts recommend a blade made of high carbon steel, which easily keeps an edge. You do, however, need to be vigilant against rust and corrosion.

FOLDING VS. FIXED

While a folding knife is compact and useful for a number of small tasks, and you may choose to carry one as part of your survival kit, if you have one knife, it should have a full-tang fixed blade. A folding knife has more parts that can break. Full-tang means that the blade extends through the hilt of the knife, adding to durability. Some knives have a hollow hilt or one that has other little tools or gadgets in it, but a full tang knife will be sturdier.

SERRATED VS. STRAIGHT EDGE

Some people recommend a serrated edge knife—it can be helpful in cutting rope for shelter, for example. Others recommend a knife with a straight edge that sharpens easily. Partially-serrated blades are also an option.

HILT

The knife's hilt should have a good grip and fit comfortably in your hand—if you're buying your first survival knife, you'll probably want to buy your knife in person rather than over the Internet. Note that the pommel of a survival knife can often be used as a tool in itself—to break glass in case of a car accident, for example.

TRAINING AND USE

It's not enough just to own a knife. It's vital that you know how to use one. View demonstrations on YouTube, invest in survival classes, and make sure that you practice skills such as building an emergency shelter or gutting fish—and that you practice with your non-dominant hand, in case of injury.

MAKE YOUR OWN ARROWHEADS

Arrowheads are one of the oldest ranged weapons in existence. Our ancestors used arrows to hunt big and small game for millennia. These tools are vital to staying alive in a survival situation, both in terms of self-defense and acquiring food. You can make arrowheads just like our prehistoric ancestors did, using simple tools that you can scavenge from natural settings.

FLINT KNAPPING

Ancient peoples made arrowheads using a process called "flint knapping." This technique uses rocks or stones to make your arrowheads. The primary advantage of this method is that you need supplies that are plentiful in nature. It does not need fire or a knife, and it makes an arrowhead that can be reused over and over.

Flint knapping requires a "source rock" to make the arrowhead out of and a "hammer stone" that you'll use to do the job. The process is three simple steps. First, you'll break open the source rock to get to the core. Then, you'll knock flakes of stone from the core. Finally, you'll shape these flakes into the arrowheads.

FIND A SOURCE ROCK

Finding the right stone to be your source rock may end up being the most difficult part of the project. This depends on the environment you find yourself in, of course. Mountainous areas and deserts or badlands are often full of the kinds of rocks you need for this tool. The rock must be brittle—meaning you can break it without much effort—and it should also be finely grained and have a uniform texture. If it has any small fractures, it won't work as well. Flint, chalcedony, chert, and quartzite are all good options for your source rock. If you aren't sure whether you have the right rock, trial and error will let you quickly find out. The source rock should be large enough that you'll be able to break off good-sized pieces to make arrowheads with. But it also shouldn't be so big that you can't work with it. You'll need to be able to hold it against a supporting structure like a tree or large stone while you work with it.

To find out whether you have a good candidate for a source rock, tap it with another rock made of harder stone. Listen to the sound it produces. If it produces a fairly high-pitched tone, it will probably make an excellent source rock. You can test it to see if fragments flake off when you strike it with your hammer rock. If they do, you're in business.

If rocks aren't available, you can also make arrowheads out of synthetic materials. The bottom of a glass bottle or pieces of porcelain will work. If you're using these items, you can skip to the section on how to shape your arrowheads.

Flint

Chalcedony

Chert

Quartzite

FIND A HAMMER STONE

The hammer stone is the tool you will need to flake off pieces of the source rock. Hammer stones should be harder than the stone in your source rock. You'll want to use a stone that is round and can be easily gripped in one hand. Stone Age people used rocks like these to do all kinds of complex tasks. They're a good tool just to have on hand in general, and they're excellent for making arrowheads. You can also make a billet; this is a tool specially designed for arrowhead shaping. Billets are usually made from solid wood or antlers and have a cylindrical shape.

FIND A STRIKING SURFACE

The last component of your arrowhead factory is the platform or striking surface. This is the area of the source rock that you will be producing arrowheads from. It should be close to an edge and have an angle of less than 90 degrees, but more than about 30 degrees. The angle is key to producing the right shapes for arrowheads.

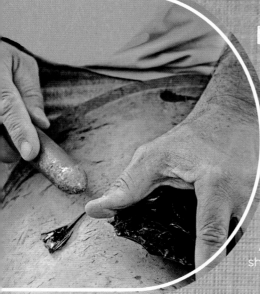

MAKE THE ARROWHEAD

To produce the arrowheads, you'll need to remove flakes of stone from your source rock. There are a couple of ways you can go about doing this. The first is to sit on the ground with your legs apart, and grip the source rock against one thigh. The second method is to crouch next to a tree or boulder and grip the source rock against its base. You can choose the method you are most comfortable with. Then, with hard, glancing blows, strike the platform to break off medium-sized pieces. These should be larger than the size of the arrowheads you eventually want to produce. After you have about a dozen, you can start shaping them into arrowheads.

PRESSURE FLAKING

A pressure flaking tool is vital to shaping arrowheads, whether you are making them from stone or from synthetic materials like glass or porcelain. Hold the pressure flaking tool against one edge of the flake of stone from your source rock. Then, in a slow, controlled manner, chip small pieces off of the stone flake. Push the pressure flaking tool against the flake below its center line, and chip a piece of the rock off. Then, flip the arrowhead over and repeat on the opposite side. Arrowheads should be symmetrical for the best effect. Continue to remove small chips of stone from the flake of rock until it is shaped into a triangle with a sharp point.

MAKE NOTCHES

Lastly, make notches at the base of the arrowhead so you can tie it to the shaft of your arrows. You can use your pressure flaking tool to make rough notches, and carve them to make them deep enough to attach to the arrows.

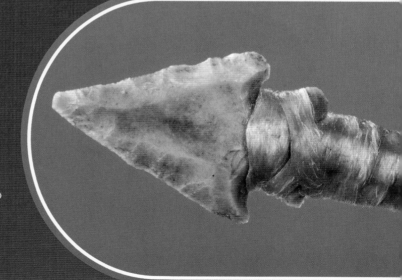

CHAPTER 3:
HOME & SURROUNDINGS

FIRE

We think of our homes as our sanctuaries, protecting us from the outside world and its dangers. But our houses, too, can be fragile. While the U.S. Fire Administration calculated that in 2016, outdoor fires were predominant, accounting for more than 558,000 instances, there were still more than 360,000 residential fires. In addition, there were more than 200,000 vehicle fires and 95,000 nonresidential fires. Knowing how to handle fires in your home is crucial.

SMOKE ALARMS

You probably have smoke alarms in your house—but how much attention do you pay to them? One question is whether you have them in the right locations, and whether you maintain them properly. Make sure that your smoke alarms have battery backup and that they are wired to respond together—that is, if a smoke alarm goes off in the basement, you should hear it in the bedroom as well. Install a smoke alarm on each level of your house and in each sleeping area. Set a reminder on your phone to test them monthly, and swap batteries once a year. Smoke alarms—as well as carbon monoxide alarms—have expiration dates, too. In general, replace them every 7–10 years.

PREVENTION

In 2016, cooking fires accounted for about half of residential fires. So be safe in the kitchen! Don't leave your oven or burners unattended, don't leave flammable materials like loose towels near the stove, and keep matches or butane lighters stored up high and out of the reach of children. Don't leave candles or space heaters unattended, and don't smoke in bed.

Make sure your address is clearly marked, so that first responders can find it easily. Have—and know how to use—a fire extinguisher. Know what materials the fire extinguisher can be used on.

HAVE A FIRE PLAN

Sit down as a family and make an evacuation plan for fires. Your kids should know how to get out of each room in the house. Do you know how to remove or get out of windows quickly? Make a plan for who will check in and help kids, anyone with mobility issues, and pets, and make sure to set a designated meetup point for the family. And don't just talk about the plan: Make it into a drill, so you can build muscle memory. Practice the drill in each season, and make sure your kids aren't just evacuating but evacuating safely. And if you have a two-story building, invest in a rescue ladder and train in its use.

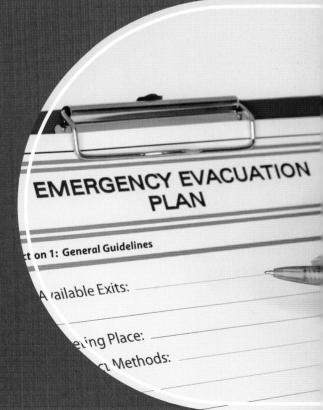

THE FIRST MOMENTS

Call 9-1-1 immediately. For a small fire, if you have a fire extinguisher nearby and training in how to use it, you can try to extinguish the fire. If the fire doesn't respond immediately, though, that's your sign to evacuate. Don't attempt to fight a fire yourself if you don't have an exit at your back, if the fire seems serious, or it's a smoky fire.

For a grease fire, don't try to quench the flames with water, which will make matters worse. Don't try to move a flaming pan off a burner, either. If you can without endangering yourself, turn off the burner and put a lid on the pan.

SAFE EVACUATION

If you are caught in a fire, follow your route to the exit and the predetermined meeting point. Stay low to the ground as you move, covering your mouth with something like a pillowcase to avoid smoke inhalation. Test any doors before you open them by touching the back of your hand to the knob. If it's hot, don't use that route. If you can, close doors behind you, as that may help stall the fire.

Convene at the meeting point. Never return to a burning building.

IF YOU CAN'T EVACUATE

If your path to safety is blocked, close any doors you can between you and the fire. Seal the doors and air vents with towels—wet, if possible—to reduce smoke in your room. Stay low near the window and alert fire personnel to your location by waving a bright cloth.

STOP, DROP, AND ROLL

Your kids likely learned this mantra in school. You may have as well! If your clothing catches on fire, do not panic or run. Instead, drop the floor and roll, smothering the fire. Do make sure that children understand that stop, drop, and roll only happens when fire strikes in person—that is, if they are evacuating a room that the fire hasn't reached yet, they don't need to drop and roll, only crawl, as they leave.

HOME INTRUDER

You return home from a day at work, only to find your door cracked open. Did you slip up that morning, or is someone inside? You wake up at night, only to hear rustling downstairs—and your spouse is already asleep beside you. How can you deal with a home intruder?

GUARD YOUR HOME

Make your home less attractive to intruders. Security bars on your lower level or basement windows can help, as can an alarm system. Do check whether the status of your alarm system can be seen from the house's exterior; you don't want a prospective burglar to see through frosted glass that your alarm system is deactivated. Dogs are also a deterrent to intruders. If you will be gone on vacation, make sure a neighbor is checking in regularly, and set up your lights to turn on in the evenings (ideally, not at the same time each evening). If you are returning home and think your home may have been robbed, back out of your driveway. Go to a neighbor's house and call the police from there. The intruders may still be in the house.

DEAL WITH STRANGERS

Practice common sense when letting someone into your home. Vet any strangers who come to your door carefully. If they try to push past your boundaries or do not respect your wariness of strangers, do not let them in. After someone has been in your house, such as a contractor, make sure all doors and windows are locked behind them. If you've given keys to a contractor, change the locks after the job is done.

HAVE A PLAN

Discuss with your family what you will do if a home invader strikes your home. In general, experts recommend against confrontation. Instead, retreat as a family to a designated "safe room" with a locking door. A code word or phrase can alert the family to put the plan in place without alerting the intruder. Once in the safe room, call 911 and alert police to the situation. If you have your car keys, set off your car's panic button.

Stock the room with water, a first aid kit, and a weapon such as pepper spray or a bat. Stay silent while you wait for the police to arrive. (Even if you think you heard the intruder leave, though, do not leave the safe room until the police have arrived.) If you can evacuate through a window, do so. If the intruder comes to you, be prepared to fight.

CONFRONTATION

A self-defense course can help you know how to incapacitate an intruder. Weapons can also be an option. If you opt for a gun, make sure that you go through proper safety training—and that you know any relevant laws in your state and city.

EARTHQUAKES

If you're Californian, you're probably used to the fact that you can't always trust the ground beneath your feet. If you grew up elsewhere in the United States, the idea may come as a shock. Faults are found throughout the United States, though, so even if you're in Tornado Alley or a coastline more prone to hurricanes, it's worth a bit of time to know how to deal with quakes.

PREPARE YOUR HOUSE

Take a tour of your house. What could fall, if the earth shook? Are heavy objects stored on lower shelves? How secure are wall hangings and overhead light fixtures? Would a hanging lamp strike a window if it swung in an earthquake? Is your television prone to toppling? (If you have small children, an unsecured TV can be a grave risk even aside from earthquakes.) Does your insurance cover earthquake damage? Take photographs of the contents of your household, especially high-value items, and make sure that your household inventory is kept in a safe place with other important documents.

If hanging lamps swing around, what will they hit?

Water heaters are tremendously heavy and prone to fall. When they do, gas and electric connections can snap, increasing the risk of fire or electric shock. Secure your water heaters carefully.

DO A FAMILY DRILL

Go through each room with your family. If you were in this room when the earthquake struck, where would be the safest place to ride out the earthquake? Have a bug out bag prepared for the aftermath, and discuss a family meetup point. If you have time before evacuation, turning off switches and utility valves is recommended. Discuss who should take responsibility for that task.

IF YOU'RE INSIDE

You may have once heard that in case of an earthquake, you should make your way to a doorway. In modern homes, that advice no longer holds true. Instead, the slogan is, "Drop, Cover, and Hold On." Drop to your hands and knees—you want to stay low but also be able to move. Seek cover under a piece of low, sturdy furniture such as a table or desk. If there isn't one nearby, move to an interior wall. Steer clear of taller furniture that may fall on you, as well as windows or cabinets that contain glassware. Cover your head and neck with your arms. If you've made it to sturdy furniture, hold onto it, as it may shift with the quake. And if you're in bed—stay there! Hold your pillow over your head for extra protection. If you're in a kitchen, try to turn off the stove before seeking a safe place.

DROP

COVER

HOLD

IF YOU'RE OUTSIDE

If you're outdoors, don't try to move inside. If you're hiking in a rocky area, stay alert for rocks and landslides. If you're in a car, pull over and stop as soon as possible. However, do not stop on an overpass or under one. Avoid areas where something may fall on your car such as utility wires, crumbling buildings, and trees. Do not park immediately next to a building, as its windows and exterior walls may topple.

AFTER THE QUAKE

Aftershocks may soon follow the initial quake— and they may even be more severe. If your building is damaged, evacuate. In multi-story buildings, do not use an elevator to do so. Make your way to your household's pre-established meeting point with your bug out bag. Do not go back inside a damaged building. Earthquakes can cause gas leaks, so do not use matches or lighters in the aftermath.

As earthquakes can cause tsunamis, if you're on a coastline, move inland or upward.

If you're trapped in rubble, text, use a rescue whistle, or bang pipes in order to alert rescuers to your location.

THUNDERSTORMS

Every spring, thunderstorms reliably come to parts of the United States. Lightning strikes and high winds can cause a lot of damage and injuries.

BEFORE THE THUNDERSTORM STRIKES

Heavy storms can knock down trees, so keep an eye on trees near your house or driveway as they grow. Keep nearby trees trimmed or cut them down altogether. Make sure your electronics are protected by surge protectors. Keep your cell phone charged so that you don't have to use a landline in a thunderstorm; electricity can travel through the wires, making landlines an electric shock risk.

IF YOU'RE INSIDE

Lightning can travel through plumbing, so don't decide that a thunderstorm is the perfect time for a leisurely soak in the bath. And if the power goes out, rely on flashlights rather than candles, which are a fire risk.

IF YOU'RE OUTSIDE

If you can avoid driving in a thunderstorm, do so. If you're already driving when one happens unexpectedly, stop at a gas station or restaurant and go inside. If there are no buildings nearby, stay in your car with the windows rolled up, keeping your body away from any metal in your car. Golf carts and motorcycles are lightning risks: Stay away from them in a thunderstorm. Equally, avoid open structures such as gazebos or playground equipment. You may want to escape the torrent, but they can draw lightning. Instead, crouch down to the ground. This makes yourself a smaller, shorter target but means that less of your body touches the ground.

TORNADOES

Where thunderstorms rage, tornadoes can follow, leaving a swath of destruction in their wake. A house on one side of the street can escape unscathed, while a house on the other is reduced to rubble.

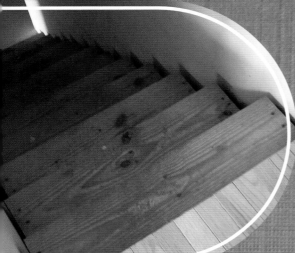

PREPARATION

Children at schools in tornado-prone areas do tornado drills. Perform them at home as well. Discuss with your family where you should go if a tornado warning goes into effect. (Note that tornado watch indicate that a tornado might develop, giving you time to prepare and watch carefully. Tornado warnings indicate a funnel has been spotted in your vicinity.) If you have a basement or cellar, plan to go there. If you do not, go to an interior room, ideally without windows. If you're in a multi-story building such as a condominium, plan to go to a hallway.

IF YOU ARE INSIDE

Once you have made it to a safe location in the building, get under something such as a table if you can, for extra protection. Cover your head and neck with a pillow, blanket, or even your hands. Avoid being near heavy furniture that might topple in high winds—in fact, think through the layout of the furniture on the floor above you; you don't want to be underneath anything heavy that might fall through in the event of ceiling collapse.

IF YOU ARE OUTSIDE

If you are outside when a tornado strikes, cover your head and neck with your arms. A coat or a blanket that you keep in your car can also provide a bit of extra protection. If you are driving, do not try to drive ahead of the tornado. Stop driving, though make sure your car isn't under or on an overpass or bridge. You might think you would be safer underneath your car, but that is actually more dangerous.

IN THE AFTERMATH

Have a plan for contacting family members to ensure that everyone is safe. Be prepared to administer first aid. In the aftermath, watch for fallen power lines. People commonly injure themselves after tornadoes while cleaning up rubble—injuries such as stepping on nails, for example. Make sure your tetanus shot is up to date, and take care to wear sturdy clothing and shoes during the cleanup phase.

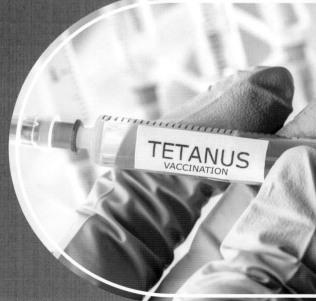

STRANDED IN A SNOWSTORM

When you're inside and you don't need to go anyplace, a snowstorm can be delightful. You cuddle up, enjoy some hot chocolate, and watch a movie. It gets more complicated when the power goes out, or you're stranded on the side of the road in your vehicle. Then, the snow that seems so soft and fluffy and beautiful abruptly turns threatening.

HOME: PREPARATION

As winter approaches, be prepared for power outages. Make sure your house is insulated as well as it can be, and that you have supplies of food and water. Make sure you have a plan for emergency heating—and that it's a safe plan. For example, if you rely on a wood stove, make sure you have a carbon monoxide detector nearby. Have flashlights in the event that the lights go out; candles are a fire risk.

DURING A COLD SNAP

Since you don't want pipes to freeze, turn on the taps a little bit. Cover any windows with blankets to conserve heat. Keep a sharp eye on children and the elderly, and have a thermometer on hand to measure their temperature in case of hypothermia. Resist the temptation to warm up with coffee or whiskey, since both caffeine and alcohol will make you get colder, faster. If you go outside to shovel the snow, take breaks. Don't try to lift too much snow at once.

CAR: PREPARATION

Stock an emergency kit in your car with water, food, warm clothes that you can layer, and blankets. Jumper cables are a must—and so is knowing how to use them. You don't want to be stopped on the side of the road, trying to learn from a smartphone with intermittent signal. Sand can help you dig your car out if it's stuck in a snowy driveway. Flashlights and emergency roadside flares can round out your kit. In addition, don't let your fuel tank drift down towards empty when it's cold outside.

ON THE SIDE OF THE ROAD

If you need to drive when snow is expected, wear layers, a coat and boots that are water-resistant, and hat, scarf, and gloves or mittens. Make sure your mobile phone is charged and that someone knows your route. If you do get stranded, tie a brightly colored cloth to your antenna to alert passerby that you need help. Make sure your exhaust pipe isn't covered with snow, averting carbon monoxide poisoning, and get your emergency supplies and blankets from the trunk. Then huddle into your emergency blankets and settle in for a wait. Stay warm by moving your arms and legs. Run your car about 10 minutes out of each hour for warmth, but crack a window as you do so to get fresh air.

FLOODING

It's been raining for days, and even after it stops, the nearby river continues to crest. You walk down to check your basement each morning with trepidation. What can you do to prepare your home for flooding, stay safe if it happens, and recover quickly?

PREVENTION

You can't prevent floods, and you can't always prevent them from affecting your home—but you can try to reduce the damage. When you're buying a home, consider its flood history. Is it in a floodway? Do you have separate flood insurance? Do you have a battery-operated sump pump for backup? Read the fine print when you buy a home; some Texas residents were horrified during Hurricane Harvey when they found that their homes were actually situated in a reservoir area that was designed to hold water. Make sure your tetanus shots are up to date.

PREPARE

If a flood is coming, gather emergency supplies. Make sure that your usual supplies of food, water, medicine, and communication devices are supplemented with waterproof boots and gloves as well as insect repellant. Bring in outdoor lawn furniture and trash cans. If you plan to weather the flood in place, gather sources of fresh water. (Note that the Red Cross cautions against using water in a bathtub as drinking water because of potential lead contamination—it can be used for other purposes such as washing clothes, however.) If you evacuate, turn off gas, power, and electricity before you go. As time permits, move valuables and furniture to higher floors.

EVACUATION

In the first chapter of the book, we discussed knowing alternate routes for evacuation. This can be especially useful in a flooding situation, where as well as traffic issues, you may face roads blocked by standing water. You don't want to drive through standing water, or be forced to drive on a bridge over rushing water.

A CAUTION

If you don't leave your home and floodwaters rise higher than you expect, while you might retreat to the higher levels of your house, do NOT go to the attic. People have been trapped in closed attics.

AFTER THE INITIAL CRISIS

Often, injuries happen after the floodwater has receded, during the cleanup process. Working in a flooded area, you must be alert for sharp debris such as nails, displaced animals that could include snakes, and electrical hazards such as downed power lines. Because floodwater can contain contaminants and chemicals, you must take care to be scrupulous about cleanliness and sanitation. Take special care with any food or eating utensils exposed to floodwater; throw even canned or sealed food out.

HURRICANES

Recent years have seen a series of destructive hurricanes in the United States. Forecasts are often chancy: People know a hurricane is coming, but not exactly where it will make landfall or how intense it will be. That makes it difficult to know when or where to evacuate. How can you best get through the situation?

SECURE YOUR HOME

During hurricane season, keep an eye on trees and bushes near your home. If any are large enough to fall and damage your home—or your neighbor's—trim or cut them down. Invest in storm shutters, or make sure you have boards on hand to board your windows. Keep your gutters unclogged.

BE PREPARED TO GO

Even if you don't end up evacuating, you don't want to be in a rush if you have to. Keep an eye on the roads and have your bug out bag packed. And keep your fuel tank close to full in hurricane season so that even if there's a run on gas, you're not affected.

BEFORE EVACUATION

Keep your house as free from damage as possible. Bring in lawn furniture and trash cans to prevent them blowing away. Board your windows. Sandbags around the doors can help guard your home—and insurance may even cover the cost if you keep your receipts. Know several potential routes for evacuation so that you can go another way if your first choice is clogged by traffic or fallen power lines. Turn off gas, power, and water before you leave, and unplug electronic devices. As time permits, put furniture and valuables on higher floors in case of flooding.

IF YOU STAY

Resist the temptation to take a photo that will make you a social media star. Stay inside, away from windows. Horribly, some people can take advantage of hurricanes to rob homes, so stay alert for intruders. Listen to reports recommending evacuation and describing the path of the storm.

AFTER THE HURRICANE

As with flooding, injuries often happen after the crisis seems to have passed. After a hurricane or flooding that results, you must be alert for sharp debris such as nails, displaced animals that could include snakes, and electrical hazards such as downed power lines. Because floodwater can contain contaminants and chemicals, you must take care to be scrupulous about cleanliness and sanitation. Take special care with any food or eating utensils exposed to floodwater; throw even canned or sealed food out. Do not let your children play with toys that have encountered floodwater.

ON THE STREET

You're walking along, enjoying the day. The only problem is, a thief or mugger is walking along too, and they want to enjoy their day at your expense. Don't be scared on the streets. Instead, take some simple steps to make yourself a less appealing target.

BE ALERT

If you're walking on the street or standing on a subway platform, don't drift into daydreams. Know how many people are around you. Look up at the streets around you, not down at your phone. If you are in an unfamiliar location as a tourist or on business, map out your route before you leave your hotel, and if you need to check your map, don't just stop on the street. Stand straight and tall as you walk. An air of confidence may help deter a mugger. If you're carrying a purse or bag, make sure it's not open. Is pricy jewelry or an expensive watch visible?

TRAVEL WITH FRIENDS

Groups are less likely to be troubled than people by themselves. Even if you are walking solo, take a route that's well-lit and full of people. If something does set off your sense of danger, don't ignore it. Duck into a café, bookstore, or restaurant.

IF YOU'RE MUGGED

Have a plan for what happens if you are mugged. Your reaction may depend on whether you have self-defense training, whether you carry a weapon such as a gun or pepper spray, and so forth. Be aware that fighting a mugger can escalate a situation. Giving a wallet—some people recommend having a "decoy" wallet or carrying relatively little cash—may get you out of the situation without harm. Regardless of whether you choose to fight back, if a mugger does target you, make some noise. And if someone tries to get you in a vehicle, at that point, fight back—even if you don't have training. Use your elbows, knees, and feet do whatever damage you can to your attacker.

AN ACTIVE SHOOTER SITUATION

Schools, theaters, concerts, and bars: All have become sites of terror and devastation. Schools have begun practicing for active shooter situations. But what if you and your family are simply out in the world: worshiping at church, buying groceries, watching a movie, or out at a park? While you can't guarantee safety, you can increase your chances of survival.

OBSERVE

When you arrive at a location, be aware of entrance and exit points. Know well the buildings you spend any amount of time in: your office, your church, your favorite restaurant. Know how you can evacuate and where you could hide.

FLEE

If you hear gunfire, leave if possible. Call 9-1-1 as soon as you are in a safe place. Get others out as you can.

HIDE

If your way out is blocked, try to find a hiding place. Silence your smartphone. Alert emergency personnel to your location through text. Turn off the lights and cover the windows. Block entrances. If you are with others, it may be tempting to cluster together in one corner of the room, but it is recommended that you spread out along the wall. Even if shooting stops or you think you hear the shooter leave, remain hidden until police come to find you in case of confusion or a second shooter.

CONFRONTING THE SHOOTER

If you have taken self-defense courses or have and know how to use a firearm, you may decide to risk confronting the shooter. Be prepared to fight aggressively. If a group of you can confront the shooter, you stand a better chance. Improvise weapons that keep you as far away from the shooter as possible, throwing books, furniture, and so forth. Stay aware of your surroundings so that if police arrive, you are not mistaken for the shooter or do not end up caught in crossfire.

FIRST AID

Take a first aid course. Know how to apply direct pressure to wounds to stop bleeding, how to treat people who may be suffering from shock, and how to use a tourniquet.

IN THE AFTERMATH

If you or a family member is involved in an active shooter situation, it can be deeply traumatizing. A support group can help, or therapy. Because conspiracy theories can abound, be careful about what information is publically available about you or your family members.

DOG ATTACK

Dogs are man's best friend—except when they aren't. Aggressive and ill-trained dogs can get off their leash or away from their enclosure and attack you or your family. Know how to fight them off and escape serious injury.

PREVENTION

If you're walking through your neighborhood or in a park and see a neighbor walking a dog you know to be aggressive, avoid that pathway. If you do encounter an aggressive dog that seems like it might attack, try to defuse the situation. You want to stay calm and hit a balance where you are neither confrontational nor running away. Stand still, hands curled into loose fists. Don't make eye contact, but don't turn your back on the dog, either. Instead, stand sideways, eyeing the dog from your peripheral vision. Don't make sudden movements—waving your arms to scare the dog may actually provoke it into attacking. If you have a walking stick or cane, don't swing it at the dog while the dog is weighing whether to attack.

FIGHTING BACK

If a dog does not lose interest and move away, command it to Sit in as deep a voice as you can. If that does not work and the dog does attack you, yell for help. Try to get something between you and the dog: a backpack, a book, a coat, a stick. If they are biting something else, their teeth won't be in you. When fighting a dog, be aware that they have thick skulls, so hitting there, even with an improvised weapon such as a stick, won't do much and may enrage them further. Their nose and throat are weaker points.

IF YOU ARE BITTEN

Try to stay standing. If you do fall, curl up and protect your face, neck, and vital organs. While the instinct to pull away if you are bitten is strong, resist it—that will further injure you. Pushing into the bite may actually cause the dog to release its jaws.

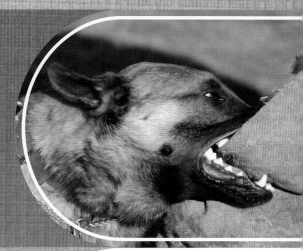

AN UNEXPECTED WEAPON

One unlikely tool if you are witness to a dog attack from your home or car is a fire extinguisher. You don't need to get close to the attack to use one, and they will interrupt many attacks.

DOG BITES

Apply basic first aid to any wounds, cleaning them and applying pressure. Talk to your doctor about whether you should have a series of rabies shots.

CHAPTER 4:
THE NATURAL WORLD

LOST IN THE WILD

So you planned for a nice hike of a few hours in the woods. Then you got lost, or sustained an injury that prevents you from walking without pain. What should you do?

BEFORE YOU LEAVE

Your ability to survive in the wilderness starts at home. Make sure you bring along a map of the area—and that you look over it carefully before you go. Bring along, and know how to read, a compass; don't rely solely on a GPS device that may lose signal. Pack a whistle, a small mirror that can catch and reflect the light, a method to start fire, a water-resistant blanket, and spare food and water. Don't forget a compact first aid kit. Check the weather forecast before you leave, and make sure that family or friends know where you are going, your expected hiking route, and when you are expected back, so they can raise the alarm if you don't return at the expected time.

AS YOU HIKE

As you hike, keep an eye out for landmarks. Look behind you every so often, so you can see what the trail looks like going the other way. Snap quick pictures of the trail so you have a visual record of your route. Take care of your body as you hike, harboring your energy so you don't get exhausted. Take breaks to drink water so you don't get dehydrated. Don't push on despite injury. If you can, rest in the shade when you stop to eat.

S.T.O.P.

Alas, despite your preparation, you find yourself lost and confused, and maybe panicking a bit. The acronym S.T.O.P. is commonly taught for that moment. S stands for Stop. If you think you're lost, don't keep wandering further in an attempt to find your way. Instead, stop so you can rest, get over any instinctive panic response, and plan. T stands for Think. When did you last recognize a landmark? How long have you been hiking, and at what speed? O stands for Observe. Do you spot any landmarks? Can you match them to your map? What direction are you facing? What time is it, and what is the weather like? P stands for plan. Should you try to retrace your steps, perhaps by following pictures you took? Should you try to signal for help? Should you sit tight and find shelter and food? If it's late in the day, or if you're tired or injured, staying in place is almost always the safest choice.

If you do choose to leave your location, for example if it's earlier in the day and you have a fairly good idea of where you're at, mark your route with small piles of stones or branches so you know if you end up walking in circles. Walking downhill will often get you closer to people. Keep a sharp eye out for signs of your initial passage.

SIGNALING FOR HELP

If you choose to wait for help, you can make it easier for people to find you with visual and auditory methods. Packing a whistle—there are ones made for survival situations—can save your voice, and the noise can travel quite a distance. If you didn't bring a whistle, banging rocks together can also save your voice. You can make it easier for a plane or drone to see you by tying a brightly-colored cloth to a tree, moving a shiny, reflective object such as a mirror, or creating an SOS signal from rocks or branches.

SHELTER, WATER, FOOD

While you wait, construct an emergency shelter. Know how to purify water—and bring purification methods with you—in case your own supply of water runs out. If conditions permit, build a small fire for warmth and to signal your location.

Ideally you have packed spare food. If not, you do have some options if your stay in the woods stretches on for days. (The human body can survive without food for two weeks, so don't search for food on your first night unless you have specific training.) Unless you are an expert, steer clear of mushrooms and berries altogether. Bring along a guidebook of the area you're exploring so that you know which plants may be edible. Fish may be a good choice, and you can fish even if you haven't bought gear, as we'll see on pages 145–149.

A CRUNCHY MEAL?

Insects such as grasshoppers, crickets, earthworms, and termites can provide protein, and those four are some of your safer choices when it comes to an insect meal. In general when it comes to insects, avoid anything brightly colored such as caterpillars, as bright coloration often indicates poison, or anything that can sting you. Smelly bugs are also often dangerous.

Cook any insects you find to get rid of germs or parasites. Avoid eating their wings, legs, or heads. And though escargot might be a delicacy, steer clear of snails: Snails in the wild have a taste for poisonous plants and might transmit that poison to you, even when cooked.

BOILING WATER

When in doubt about the potability of your water supply, you can ensure its cleanliness (well, at least its "antimicrobialness") by boiling it. But if you don't have an updated wilderness manual, you may not know that boiling water for extended period of time doesn't make it any cleaner, and in fact, boiling isn't even necessary.

HOW HOT IS HOT ENOUGH?

It's a misconception that water must reach the boiling point—212 degrees Fahrenheit—to kill pathogens. The temperature needed to knock off most critters (excluding extreme varieties such as bacteria living in volcanoes) is just 185 degrees Fahrenheit. Bacteria, microbes, viruses, and parasites are killed off after just a few minutes at that temperature. Disease-causing pathogens, then, are already dead by the time the water begins to boil.

In developing countries where firewood is scarce and water is filled with bacteria, it is imperative to adhere to recommended boiling times. Since you're unlikely to have a cooking thermometer handy, the prudent route is simply to wait for the water to boil.

HOW LONG?

Yet various safety guides recommend boiling water for 5, 10, even 20 minutes. At this point much of the water will evaporate, and fuel will have been wasted. In light of criticism about wasting energy to boil water, the Centers for Disease Control and the Environmental Protection Agency lowered their suggested boiling times. Both now recommend heating water to a rolling boil for only one minute. The exception is if you are at a high altitude—if so, boil water for a minimum of three minutes.

WHY NOT WAIT?

In survival situations when fuel and water supplies are limited, waiting too long for water to boil can have dangerous repercussions. When all you have are a few pieces of firewood and water from a murky stream, sitting idly by as the water boils away may result in a long, cold, thirsty night.

Note that while boiling water removes bacteria and parasites, it doesn't remove toxic chemicals or fuels.

BUILDING AN EMERGENCY SHELTER

Shelter is one of the most basic survival requirements. Shelter can mean the difference between surviving the night or suffering from exposure. It keeps you out of the elements, keeps your gear dry, and helps conceal you from attackers and wild animals. When you're looking for a good location to build an emergency shelter, keep a few key things in mind. To start, try to use the terrain to help construct your shelter. If you're camping, try to find a spot that is protected from wind by hills or depressions in the ground. Look for caves or rock overhangs that will protect you from the elements, and carefully assess them to make sure they're safe.

TIME AND EFFORT

Consider how much time and effort you can dedicate to building your shelter. Also, think about how well you need to be protected from the elements. Your shelter requirements will be different in different seasons, climates, and weather conditions. Next, make sure you have the tools you need to build the shelter you want. If you don't have the right tools, will you be able to find or make improvised tools? Lastly, assess the available materials for building the shelter. To be able to quickly answer these questions, it's good to familiarize yourself with a few different styles of shelters and know what you'll need to make them.

LEAN-TO

A lean-to is the simplest kind of shelter. You can build one with materials you've scavenged from the environment, like tree branches, but if you keep a poncho or tarp in your go bag, you'll be better equipped to make a lean-to. A very simple one can be built with a poncho and a rope that's about three yards long. Find two trees that are about 2–3 yards apart. Check the wind direction before you start: You will want the back of the lean-to to be against the wind.

Cut your rope into equal lengths. Tie each length to one of the poncho's (or tarp's) long sides. Attach a foot-long stick to each rope, about two inches from the lean-to's corners. The stick will keep rainwater from running down the ropes and into the shelter.

Tie the other ends of the ropes to each of the trees. Spread out the lean-to, and attach it to the ground with sharp sticks. If the tarp or poncho has grommets at the corners, use them to secure the structure in place. Pile brush or rocks on either side of the lean-to for further wind and rain protection, and cover the ground with an insulating material like dried leaves or pine needles.

SIMPLE TENT

This is a step up from the lean-to. Essentially, it adds a second wall to the structure and protects you on two sides from the elements. Like the lean-to, it can be constructed with a poncho or tarp. It also has a lower silhouette than a lean-to, making it more concealed from distant observers.

To make a basic tent, you will need a poncho or tarp, two ropes about three yards long, six sharpened sticks about two feet long, and two trees about three yards apart.

Tie a 3-foot rope to the center grommets on each side of the poncho or tarp, and secure the other ends of these ropes to each of the trees at about knee height, stretching the poncho or tarp taut. Pull one side of the poncho/tarp tight to the ground and secure it by pushing a sharp stick through the grommets. Secure the sticks with heavy rocks. Repeat this on the other side. Just like with the lean-to, reinforce the sides by piling debris or gear at both ends of the tent to add protection from the wind, and scatter leaves or pine needles on the ground for insulation.

DUGOUT SHELTER

In some scenarios, you may not be able to build a tent or lean-to. The materials may not be available, or you may be in an environment where trees aren't abundant. In these situations, a dugout shelter is your best option. It is basically a hole in the ground—but it's a hole that has been reinforced to provide the best comfort and insulation from the elements.

ADVANTAGES

One of the primary advantages of a dugout shelter is that it does not require a lot of time or virtually any materials to build. A dugout is not meant to be a long-term shelter, but it will keep you warm and dry for one or two nights. In a survival scenario, that can sometimes be the difference between living and dying.

WHERE TO BUILD

As with other shelters, look for the best terrain features to give you maximum cover. Look for a depression in the ground that already provides some natural cover. Try to find a depression in higher ground rather than at the base of a long slope. This will help you prevent rainwater runoff from collecting in it.

HOW TO BUILD

Clear out the brush and debris from the depression, and save it for later use. Dig a hole in the depression that is slightly longer than your height so you can comfortably lie down in. Make sure the sides of the hole are higher than your body.

Create a roof over the dugout by positioning large branches and dead wood over the hole. Fill in gaps with smaller sticks. Pile leaves and brush on top of this layer. You can improve insulation by making a few layers of branches, brush, and leaves. Try to design the roof so it is concealed from casual observers.

SURVIVE A BEAR ATTACK

In North America, there are two species of bear—black and brown (which includes subspecies grizzly and Kodiak bears). Both types are known to attack humans, and, in the past century, approximately 100 people have died in North America due to bear attacks. In the interest of not becoming part of that "grizzly" statistic, follow these tips to avoid or survive a bear attack.

Black bear

Brown bear

PREVENTION

As you hike through bear country, keep an eye out for claw marks or droppings, and note any scratched up trees or fresh kills, such as deer. Move away from any signs of bear, not towards them. Avoid investigating dark, unknown caves or hollow logs, where bears make their dens, and avoid areas identified by scavengers, such as raccoons, as there may be a feeding bear nearby.

If you do see a bear, don't whip out your camera. Leave pictures of bears to professional wildlife photographers. Many attacks have occurred because someone decided to try to snap a photo in bear territory. Bears don't like you, and they don't want their picture taken.

LEAVE NO TRACE

If you're camping, pick up all garbage, cooking supplies, and other materials. Clean up thoroughly after meals, and secure food overnight high above the ground (by hanging it from a tree branch) to prevent it from attracting bears. Not only do sloppy campers damage the area's ecosystem, they're also more likely to come face-to-face with a bear that has followed their gravy train.

MAKE NOISE

Some experts recommend tying a bell to your foot or backpack to make noise as you travel. You can also sing or holler at your hiking buddies. Just don't be a ninja. Bears don't like to be surprised.

BE CALM AND BACK OFF

Okay, so you've spotted a bear, and the bear has spotted you. Stop right there, and don't move. Speak to the bear in a low, calm voice, and slowly raise your arms up above your head. This makes you appear larger. Don't make eye contact. Leave slowly and go back from whence you came. Don't cross the path of the bear (or any cubs, if present). Just rewind, slowly, and don't come back. This especially applies to bears with cubs. A mother bear with her cubs is not open to negotiation. She will attack if she thinks she or her cubs are in danger.

DON'T RUN

The worst thing you could do at this point would be to get out your camera or try to feed the bear a snack. The second worst thing you could do would be to run. Bears run faster than humans, and they think chasing prey is fun. Running at any point will trigger the bear's chase instinct.

PLAY DEAD?

If a bear is charging you, one option is simply to stand still. The charge may be a bluff, and if you stand your ground, the bear may go away. Another option is playing dead. Lie flat on your stomach and protect the back of your neck with your hands and your face with your elbows. This might make you seem vulnerable to the grizzly bear and he or she will sniff you, growl at you, and hopefully leave you alone. IMPORTANT: If you're dealing with a black bear, do NOT play dead. They'll be thrilled that the work's been done for them and will commence lunch. If you can't tell what kind of bear you're dealing with, don't try it! Try to put your backpack up on top of you for an extra layer of protection.

DEFENSE MECHANISMS

Many camping and national park areas don't allow firearms, so some recommend bear spray or pepper spray. But beware: If you spray halfheartedly, it will only make the bear angrier.

THE FIGHT OF YOUR LIFE

Your last option is to fight back with everything you've got. There's really no need to tell you that, at this point, you're in big trouble. Kick, scream, flail your arms, go for the eyes—do whatever you can because you're in for the fight of your life. Use sticks and rocks against the bear's snout and eyes. Try to get as much distance between you and the bear as possible; throwing is safer than a direct hit.

FISHING WITHOUT FISHING GEAR

In a survival situation, finding food is always a top priority. And if you can find food that packs a lot of high-energy protein into small servings, even better. Fish are an excellent resource for this. But what happens if you find yourself in a survival situation without any gear? In that case, you'll need to know some basic techniques for fishing without gear. This can be the difference between going hungry and staying alive. There are a few different approaches. You can make improvised fishing gear, build a fish trap called a weir, or use your bare hands to catch fish.

MAKE YOUR OWN

Improvising fishing gear will require you to be creative and resourceful enough to discover new uses for things you're carrying and items you can scavenge. You can make a fishing hook from a wide variety of objects. Nails, safety pins, and broken pieces of metal can make simple fishing hooks. So can organic materials such as antlers, shells, bones, and sticks.

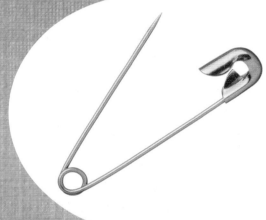

MAKING A HOOK

If you have a knife, it will make improvising a fishing hook much easier. You can make a gorge hook very quickly using a knife and a stick or other straight piece of material that can be cut safely and easily. Make a notch in the middle of the hook, and attach the line at the notch. Then, hide the gorge hook inside a piece of soft bait. When a fish swallows the bait, the gorge hook should catch in its throat, letting you reel it in.

To make a gorge hook, sharpen a small stick on both sides.

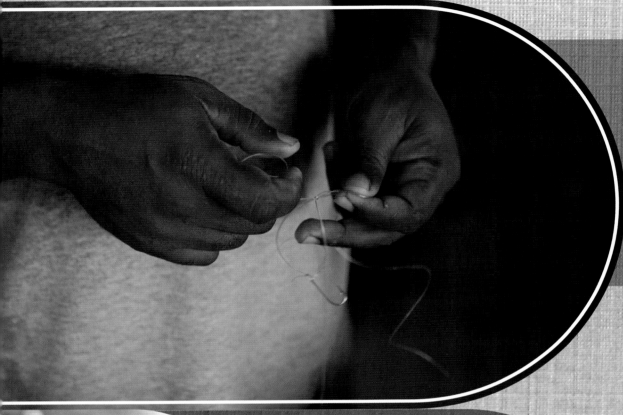

MAKING A LURE

If you choose to use a lure to entice fish, you can make it out of just about anything that is attractive or shiny. Pieces of aluminum or jewelry make excellent lures. Live bait is also a great way to catch fish without a synthetic lure. Dig for earthworms: They can be found just about anywhere there is warm, fertile soil. Insects and worms that will make good bait are often found along the banks of ponds or streams.

FISHING LINE

You can make a fishing line out of a wide variety of materials as well. Strong threads scavenged from clothing or equipment, synthetic materials such as wire or cords, and organic materials like braided grass or vines all make excellent fishing lines. While your line doesn't need to be very long for fishing in a survival situation, it does need to be strong. You do not want to spend hours making a hook, use valuable resources for bait, and spend more time fishing just to have your line snap when a hungry fish bites. In a survival situation, every minute counts and all resources are precious. Test your fishing line before using it. Tie one end of the line to a small tree and pull firmly on it to see if it is strong enough to catch a fish.

SET YOUR LINES

In a survival scenario, you won't want to spend precious time waiting for a fish to bite. While that can be a relaxing pastime, you will need to be accomplishing other tasks such as gathering firewood or building a shelter. Fortunately, you can set your fishing lines and leave them to do the work for you while you're accomplishing other tasks. A very basic way to set fishing lines is to tie them to thin tree branches that hang over the river or pond. Or you can make spring poles. To do this, cut young saplings and "plant" them in the riverbank securely and at an angle that allows the line to drop into the water. Make sure you check your lines regularly.

SPEAR FISHING

When bait or gear for making a fishing line are scarce, you can try spear fishing. To make a simple spear, you'll need a knife. Whittle one end of a short, straight branch into a sharp point. If you can, make the point barbed so that it firmly sticks in the target. If you have a flashlight or a way to make torches or candles, you can spear fish at night. The fish will be attracted to the light source, and won't be able to see you strike until it's too late. Spear fishing takes practice to get right—and obviously, practicing before you're in a survival situation is better than learning by trial or error when your life is on the line. But once you know how to do it, it has several advantages—the main one being that you can pick your targets instead of waiting for a random fish to bite.

BUILDING A WEIR

A great passive way to catch fish is by building a trap called a weir. To do this, you'll need to make or scavenge a few dozen long stakes. Plant them in the stream to make a fence shaped like the letter V. The open end should face upstream, and there should be a small opening at the vertex of the V that fish can get through. The weir works by allowing fish to swim through the V and into a small, baited enclosure at the bottom. Once they're in the trap, it will be difficult for them to swim out. You can harvest them by hand or wait by the enclosure with your spear to catch them.

NOODLING

What if, in the most extreme survival situation, you have no gear, no knife, and there aren't supplies readily available to scavenge? In this case, you can fish by hand, using a technique called noodling. Find a riverbank that is undercut by the water, overhanging rocks, or hollowed-out logs in the riverbed. These are all places where catfish and other bottom-feeders like to hang out. All you have to do is slowly and carefully reach down and grab a fish by the gills. It's not an easy technique to learn, but once you know how, you'll have an invaluable skill that allows you to get protein with zero tools.

DIY FISH CAGE TRAP

Fish traps were one of the first tools early humans developed. Prehistoric hunter-gatherer bands used them. Like most primitive tools, they're still quite useful. A solid fish trap gives the fisher many of the same advantages as hunting traps. Chief among these is the fact that you can be off doing other chores or gathering supplies elsewhere, while the trap does the work of fishing for you. With just a little time and a few of the right materials such as vines, reeds, or tree branches, you can quickly and simply build a working fish trap. In some situations, a fish trap adds a welcome source of food to a homestead. In others, it can mean the difference between life and death. Here's how you can build one using easily scavenged materials from nature.

GATHER MATERIALS

Building a fish trap does require a blade, whether it's a survival knife or a stone arrowhead. You will build it from about 30–40 dowels. These can take the form of tree branches, strong reeds, or human-fabricated materials. You will also need about 100 feet of rope, which you will either have in your survival go bag or have to make by hand from vines. Wisteria and kudzu are excellent sources of vines for this project. Cut the vines from the main plant about a week in advance of building the trap. This allows them to dry out and shrink. If you have it, thick twine or string is also helpful for this project

While kudzu vines are generally an invasive nuisance, they can prove helpful for this project.

BUILD THE OUTER SHELL

Using the thickest vines, fashion three circular hoops that are about nine or ten inches in diameter. If you have twine or string, use it to secure the ends of the hoop together. If not, you can do this with additional vines. Make sure they are tied tightly together to prevent the hoop from coming undone while fish are in the trap. Then, connect the dowels at one end to one of the hoops. Do this by weaving the hoop between the dowels and securing it with more vines. Do this again with the second hoop near the center of the dowels, and again with the third hoop at the opposite end.

CLOSE ONE END

Choose one end of the hoop—it doesn't matter which side—and close it by laying dowels across it and securing them with vines. Then weave vines through the dowels to make a mesh that is small enough that fish won't be able to escape, but porous enough that water can pass through. Secure it to the hoop using more vine, or twine if it's available.

Reeds can be used to make dowels.

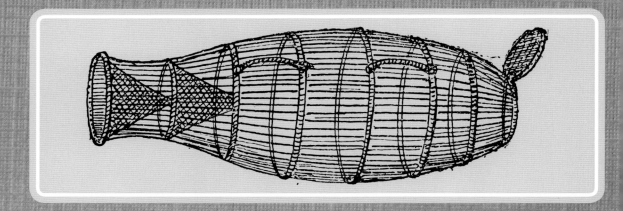

BUILD A FUNNEL

This part is the key to a successful fish trap. A cone-shaped entrance allows fish to enter the trap, but keeps them from getting out. Make a fourth hoop that is a bit smaller than the cylinder you've built. It should fit snugly into the trap. Attach short dowels at varying intervals along this hoop, securing them in place with twine or vines. Using more twine or vines, secure the open end of the dowels into an even smaller circle. You want fish to be able to squeeze through the funnel when coming in, but unable to push their way back out past the "teeth" created by the dowels. Set the funnel into the trap, teeth first, and secure it to the sides of the trap with vines or twine.

Ancient fishing equipment is still used today in rural areas.

BAIT THE TRAP

Bait the trap with meat, fish, or invertebrates. Tie it to the inside of the trap so it's floating free in the middle when you place the trap in the water. If you notice that bait is disappearing from the trap, but you aren't catching any fish, this indicates that small fish are getting in the trap and are able to get back out. If this is the case, build a little box around the bait so that fish can smell it but can't get at it.

SET THE TRAP

Secure the trap in a lake, stream, or river by placing a rock at the bottom. The trap should lie on its side so fish can easily swim in through its funnel opening. If it's in a stream or river, the opening of the trap should face upstream. The current will help make it easier for fish to enter the trap, and harder for them to get out. Check your trap regularly. If you've trapped some fish, simply remove the trap from the water, and let the fish die from lack of oxygen. Then open the funnel, dump out the fish, and enjoy a delicious, sustaining meal.

SURVIVING IN THE OCEAN

Staying alive in the open ocean, regardless of how long you need to do it, is one of the most challenging survival scenarios there is. Open water is very dangerous for many reasons. In the ocean, extreme weather is more life-threatening. There is no way to find fresh water. Risk of injury from sun exposure is very high. And the ocean is full of predators that can attack almost without warning. And yet, the ocean can be survived. We have many accounts of people staying alive for days, weeks, and even months in open water. Luck, resilience, and the proper skills and tools make such survival possible.

GET IT TOGETHER

One of the bleakest ocean survival scenarios involves floating in a life preserver out of sight of land. In this scenario, you will be totally exposed to the sun and weather. At higher latitudes the water temperature could cause you to die from hypothermia in hours. This means you need to get out of the water as quickly as you can. If your watercraft has capsized, look for pieces of wreckage you can use as a makeshift raft. Or, if you know you're within a few miles of a coast, be alert for signal buoys in the water. You may be able to pull yourself onto one and get out of the water. In a situation like this, you will want to have a life preserver equipped with a survivor locator beacon. These send a radio signal to search and rescue teams, and if you're holding on to a buoy, your position will be fixed, making rescue more likely.

FIND SHELTER

If you manage to make it out of the water, your next enemy is exposure. The sun can quickly dehydrate, burn, and cause heat exhaustion. To minimize the risks of this, cover any exposed skin with clothing. If you can, build a lean-to shelter to provide shade. Do whatever you have to do to stay out of the sun.

FIND WATER

Even if you are staying out of the sun, an ocean environment can still quickly dehydrate you simply because it's so salty. Finding drinkable water is critical to your survival. It's a terrible situation to be in: suffering from dehydration while surrounded by water, all of which will kill you if you drink it. In this scenario, your best option is to hope for rain. You'll need to be prepared to collect rainwater and store it on your raft. At sea, storms can move in very rapidly. Being ready for them is your best bet for getting drinkable water.

FIND WHERE YOU ARE

One of the best-case ocean survival scenarios is when you're in a life raft that has a means of piloting it, whether by outboard motor, sail, or oars. But that's only half the battle. You will need to navigate the craft as well. Just having a compass can mean the difference between finding land or not. But a Global Positioning System (GPS) device is much better. If you have a GPS system and a radio, you can send your coordinates to search-and-rescue teams. What if you don't have a compass or a GPS system? In that case, you might be able to navigate using stars and the sun. But you'll need to know how to do it. Therefore, it's a good idea to learn how to navigate with celestial bodies before you put to sea. If you're going on a long voyage, find out where the commercial shipping lanes are in your area. That way, you can navigate towards them in hope of being picked up.

FIND FOOD

While the ocean is teeming with life, food is very scarce at its surface. But if you're adrift for any length of time, you will have to find food. You might be able to fish if you have equipment to do so. It will be difficult, but it can lead to other sources of food. You can attract hungry seabirds with fish you catch, and you may be able to catch and kill them for food as well. But both of these scenarios are high risk and low reward. It's best to ensure that you have rations secured aboard life rafts or in survival preservers long before you'll ever need them.

PLAN AHEAD

Ultimately, your odds of success increase exponentially if you are already prepared for surviving in open water before you have to do so. That means your boat should have life rafts that are fully stocked with survival gear and supplies, and that can hold everyone onboard the craft. Make sure your rafts or survival gear includes satellite phones, ship-to-shore radios, and infrared signal beacons to contact search-and-rescue teams. Take classes to familiarize yourself with navigational techniques, open-water fishing, and other skills you'll need to survive. If you have the right tools and expertise, with a bit of luck and preparation you can survive any survival scenario—even one as risky as the open ocean.

SURVIVE A SHARK ATTACK

Shark attacks are rare—in the United States, there are generally fewer than twenty a year, and many of those are not fatal. Nonetheless, if you're swimming in the ocean, it's good to take some common sense steps to avoid becoming a statistic.

WHICH SHARKS?

Three species of shark are responsible for most human attacks: great white, tiger, and bull sharks. A hammerhead might freak you out, but it probably won't bite you.

Great white shark

Tiger shark

Bull shark

PREVENTION

Sharks see contrast well, so wearing bright colors like yellow and orange is not a great idea. Also avoid shiny jewelry as sharks may mistake it for fish scales. If you're menstruating, stick to the sand. Blood attracts sharks. Female or male, if you cut yourself on a reef or a rock while swimming, it's best to get out right away—the smell of blood to a shark is like the smell of fresh doughnuts to humans.

LOCATION, LOCATION, LOCATION

If you don't want to tangle with a shark, don't go where sharks hang out. If you plan to vacation near the ocean, contact local tourism offices and ask for shark stats in the area. When you're in the water, avoid areas inshore of sandbars or between sandbars. This is where sharks most often gather to find their prey.

SWIM SMART

Always swim with a buddy, and don't swim at dusk or at night. Sharks don't have the best vision, so when it's dark, you look like dinner to them. Keep an eye out for the behavior of other animals. Creatures of the sea know much more about the waters than you ever will. So, if turtles and fish start freaking out, there's probably a reason. Take a cue from those who have seen it before and take off. Speaking of animals, allowing dogs to swim in the ocean can be dangerous if you're in shark territory. Animals swim erratically, attracting the attention of sharks. Don't let pets stay in the water for long periods of time.

SEE A SHARK? SHOUT!

If there's a dorsal fin on the horizon, letting people know is a good idea. The more people know what's going on, the better off you are if the situation worsens. Then quickly swim toward shore as if your life depends on it...because it just might.

FIND SOMETHING SOLID

A zigzagging shark is looking for angles, so you can back up against a reef, a piling, or some other kind of outcropping, do so. This reduces the number of angles the shark has to come at you. If you're in open water, get back-to-back with your swimming buddy. You do have a swimming buddy, right?

FIGHT BACK

If a shark is circling you, that means it's about to strike. Time to fight back! It might sound ridiculous, but try to stay calm. If you're being attacked by a shark, go for the eyes and gills, the most vulnerable parts of the shark. If you can wound the eyes, you've got a chance. Use anything you have to make your strike: a surfboard, scuba gear, or, as a last resort, your fist. If you're feeling wily, you can even try getting your hands into the gill openings to really cause the shark some pain. Remember that a shark is a predator and its instinct is to attack vulnerable prey, so keep fighting. If you can show it that you are not defenseless, it's more likely to move on to an easier target.

WHAT NOT TO DO

Don't play dead. This does nothing but make the shark think it has won. The shark will then commence chomping. Clearly, this is not what you want it to do. Also, if you've been attacked, get away as fast as you possibly can. Sharks smell blood. You didn't fare too well with the first one and there are probably more on the way.

AVALANCHE

You're on the slopes when you, or someone near you, triggers an avalanche. Snow is tumbling towards you, and you know that once it settles you'll feel like you're trapped in concrete. In an avalanche situation, seconds can count. How can you maximize your chances for survival?

PREVENTION AND PREPARATION

As always, preparation is key. If you're going to be skiing in the back country, take an avalanche safety course. Don't just assume that you're going to be okay—examine the weather conditions and think through your risks. Periods of heavy snowfall, high winds, and sudden changes of temperature can all increase the chances of an avalanche. Recent avalanches in the area heighten the chances that there will be more. Pay attention to both avalanche advisories and the snow beneath your feet. If it's cracking or collapsing, that is a huge sign of danger. And know your slope. A slope meter can help you determine which slopes to avoid: 90 percent of avalanches occur on slopes between 30 and 45 degrees.

GEAR TO HAVE

There are multiple items in which you can invest that can save your life in an avalanche situation. A rescue beacon is probably the most important. Wear it immediately beneath your coat, and make sure it works before you set off. An old technology, avalanche cords can be a simple backup for your rescue beacon; they trail behind you, and if you are caught in an avalanche, odds are good that part of the cord will stay above the snow and signal your position to rescuers. Avalanche probes and shovels can help you dig out and rescue others. If you have more money and ski frequently, you may want to invest in an avalanche airbag system.

Avalanche probe

THE FIRST FEW SECONDS

Your reaction in the first few seconds of an avalanche can save your life. If you are the one who triggers the avalanche and see the snow cracking beneath you, try to jump above the slab you're on. If you're beneath the point of the avalanche and see it moving toward you, move sideways. Even if you are not able to avoid the avalanche altogether, you may be able to avoid the most dangerous central volume of snow. If there are nearby trees, try to hang on to one—although in a larger avalanche, the tree itself may be ripped away from the slope.

IN THE AVALANCHE

If you are caught in the avalanche, you want to try to stay near the top. Experts recommend "swimming," moving your arms and legs as if you were trying to keep yourself from drowning in water. Of course, swimming requires a lot of coordination when you're being pushed down a slope by a great volume of snow, but even thrashing can be helpful. Experts also recommend keeping one arm pointed "upward" (spitting can help you determine direction) to help rescuers find you.

BEFORE THE SNOW SETTLES

As you come to a stop, you want to give yourself as much air and time as possible. Cupping your mouth and digging a hole around your face will give you more oxygen. Take a deep breath, expanding your chest to give yourself room to breathe, before the snow settles. Trying to punch your hand to the surface can both help generate a pathway for air and let rescuers see where you are. If you can't dig your way to the surface easily, it's better to conserve your energy and oxygen and wait for rescue than to struggle fruitlessly.

FOREST FIRES

Sparked by lightning or careless fireworks or cigarettes, wildfires can spread quickly. One moment, you're enjoying an afternoon hike. The next, you're trying to get back to safety. Here are some tips for what to do—and what not to do.

PREVENTION

Especially in the western United States, check the fire safety level before you go hiking. Respect any burn bans. If you are allowed to start a campfire, make sure you watch it carefully. Extinguish it fully before sleeping or leaving your camp site. Be careful when you discard matches or extinguish cigarettes. If you are visiting an area at risk of wildfires, pack a fire blanket in your gear.

EVACUATION

If you are asked to evacuate, follow orders. Move downward, not upward, as fires climb up slopes. Head towards lower areas and try to stay near water. Leafy greens will burn more slowly than grasses or evergreens, so sticking close to them will provide a small measure of protection. If you encounter a blaze, try to submerge yourself in a pond or stream. Stay under even after the fire passes if you can to avoid the heated air. If water is not available, lie in a depression underneath wet clothing—as long as it's made of natural material, not nylon. Lie face down as the fire passes.

CHAPTER 5:
FIRST AID

FIRST AID OVERVIEW

In this section, we suggest some remedies for minor common problems when you're not able to get to a grocery store or see a doctor. However, for more serious issues, such as heart attack, stroke, burns, bleeding, or choking, we recommend you take a first aid course. To be truly prepared for emergencies, you can't just read a book on first aid or stock a medical reference book in your house and car. Instead, take a training course through a local community center or emergency services, the American Heart Association, or the Red Cross. At a training course, you can not only read but practice your skills. At a training course, you can also learn when to seek further help—though in a crisis situation, that help may come from a neighbor or community member rather than a medical facility.

STAY UP TO DATE

The other key is to keep your skills up to date. Take a refresher or recertification course every three years. If you learned CPR a few decades ago in high school, for example, you may find that the techniques have changed over time. Not only will this keep your skills sharp, but it may put you in touch with people in your community with whom you can pool resources in a time of crisis.

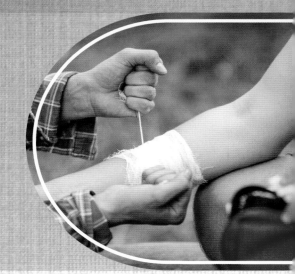

BITES AND STINGS

With billions of bugs out there, you're bound to be bitten or stung sometime in your life—and it might be at the worst time, when you can't run to an urgent care facility because they're overwhelmed. Typically, the worst reactions are to bees, yellow jackets, hornets, wasps, and fire ants. Other nasty creatures, such as blackflies, horseflies, black or red (not fire) ants, and mosquitoes, also bite and sting, but their venom usually does not cause as intense a reaction. No matter what attacks, once you're zapped, the body reacts with redness, itching, pain, and swelling at the bite site. These symptoms may last for a few minutes or a few hours.

PREVENTION

Cover your feet! Don't go barefoot in the grass; it's a favorite nesting, resting, and grazing ground for insects.

Cover up! Wear long-sleeved shirts and long pants outside to reduce skin exposure.

Take care around the clothesline. Flying, stinging insects can get caught in the laundry and be brought inside.

Don't look or smell like a flower. Bright, floral clothing and perfumes, lotions, and hair sprays can attract stinging insects.

A wasp's nest.

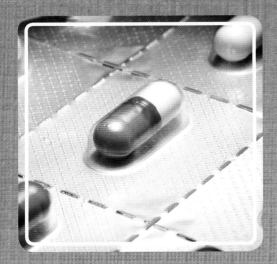

ANTIHISTAMINES

Keep over-the-counter antihistamines in your stocked first aid kit. They can help an itchy bite, since the itch is really a mild allergic reaction. However, do not take an antihistamine if you are sensitive to these medications, have allergies to ingredients in the products, are taking a conflicting medication, or are pregnant.

ACTIVATED CHARCOAL

This can help draw out the toxins that cause inflammation, swelling, and itching. To make a paste, open 2 to 3 capsules of charcoal, mix with enough water to make a paste, and apply to the affected area. After 30 minutes, wipe the paste off with a wet cloth.

BAKING SODA

Itching can be tamed by applying a paste of 3 teaspoons baking soda to 1 teaspoon water directly to the site. This remedy is especially good for ant bites and bee stings, both of which are acidic in nature.

REMOVE THE STINGER

Bees and yellow jackets leave evidence behind when they strike: their barbed stinger. It's not a pleasant sight to see this pulsating barb puncturing the skin and releasing venom. Carefully and gently remove the stinger by scraping it off with the flat edge of a knife, credit card, playing card, or fingernail. Don't reach for the tweezers or tongs. Squeezing and grabbing the stinger causes more venom to be pumped into the victim. After removing the stinger, apply a topical antiseptic.

ONION

Get a tissue, a knife, and an onion for this sting remedy. An onion (or garlic clove) contains antibiotic and anti-inflammatory substances that minimize infections and swelling from bites and stings. Slice the onion in half, and hold the onion on the bite site for five to ten minutes.

BLEEDING

Your first aid kit should contain sterile bandages and disposable gloves. Wearing the gloves, help the person lie down and move any clothing away from the wound. Don't try to remove any debris that's embedded in the wound, though do remove stray debris if you can.

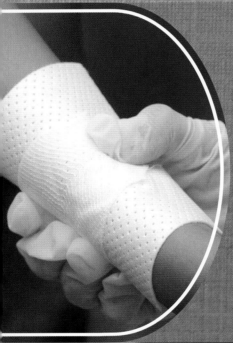

PRESSURE

Especially for more serious bleeding, stopping the bleeding is more important than cleaning out the wound, so apply bandages and pressure as soon as possible without stopping to clean the wound first. Press the bandage to the wound and apply pressure until the bleeding stops. Note that sanitary napkins should be stocked in your first aid kit, as they can act as good pressure bandages in a pinch. When bleeding has stopped, you can gently clean the wound with soap and water and secure bandages with adhesive tape. The exceptions to this rule are bites and punctures wounds; they should be left unbandaged. Keep the person still and elevate the limb above the heart if possible. Seek medical attention if at all possible.

Tourniquets can be useful, but only apply one if you have training.

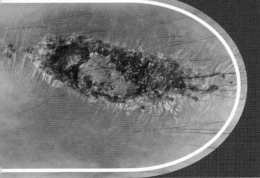

FURTHER DANGERS

Keep an eye on the patient for any indications that the wound has become infected. The symptoms of sepsis include shivering, clammy skin, pain, fever, and disorientation.

CARBON MONOXIDE

Carbon monoxide is colorless, odorless—and deadly. Unfortunately, it can be produced by common methods of heating such as burning propane, natural gas, charcoal, or gasoline. For example, camp stoves and generators, when improperly used, can both be sources of carbon monoxide poisoning. If you are using a generator, camp stove, or lantern in an emergency situation, you must make sure it's vented properly. Running generators in basements or sheds is not recommended, nor is using a charcoal grill or camp stove inside a camper or tent. Maintain a carbon monoxide detector in your home and camper, and make sure it's battery powered so that it will still be useful when the power goes out.

Never run your car inside a garage to keep warm. And err on the side of caution: even if you open the garage door, don't run your car inside the garage.

SYMPTOMS AND TREATMENT

Headaches, weakness, dizziness, and confusion are all symptoms of carbon monoxide poisoning. Blurred vision and nausea are also common. Eventually, loss of consciousness can result. If you are experiencing these symptoms, the best thing you can do is to get into fresh air immediately. Then seek medical advice.

DEHYDRATION

Every cell in your body needs water in order to function properly. In fact, an adult's body weight is 60 percent water while an infant's is as much as 80 percent water. By the time you feel thirsty, you've already lost 1 percent of your body's total water. And other than oxygen, there's nothing that your body needs more than water.

HOW WE LOSE WATER

Each and every time you exhale, water escapes your body—up to as much as 2 cups per day. It evaporates invisibly from your skin—another 2 cups per day. And you urinate approximately 2 1/2 pints every 24 hours. Add it up, and you could be losing up to 10 cups of water every day, and that's before you break a sweat. Seniors are particularly prone to dehydration, as they have a decreased sense of thirst.

Because water has so many life-sustaining functions, dehydration isn't just a matter of being a little thirsty. The effects depend on the degree of dehydration, but a water shortage causes your kidneys to conserve water, which in turn can affect other body systems. You'll urinate less and can become constipated. As you become increasingly more dehydrated, these symptoms will develop: diminished muscular endurance, dizziness, lack of energy, decreased concentration, drowsiness, irritability, headache, tachycardia (galloping heart rate), increased body temperature, collapse, permanent organ damage, or death.

HOW MUCH IS ENOUGH?

Obviously, you don't want to develop the problems listed here, so you have to ask: How much water do I need each day? Under normal conditions, the standard of 64 ounces per day is sufficient. That amount includes water from sources other than the tap. If you're spending a lot of time out in the sun sweating, you'll probably need more. A good way to tell if you're adequately hydrated is by observing the color of your urine. If it's dark yellow or amber, that's a sign that it's concentrated, meaning there's not enough water in the wastes that are being eliminated. If it's light (the color of lemon juice) that's normal.

Bathroom breaks should happen every two to three hours. If you don't need to urinate for longer periods of time, you're not drinking enough water. The simple cure for dehydration comes from water. Make sure you keep purified and filtered water in adequate supply. But there are other helpers that will keep you hydrated too.

Bananas
They have great water content and are especially good for restoring potassium that has vanished with dehydration.

Bland Foods
If you've experienced dehydration, stick to foods that are easily digested for the next 24 hours because stomach cramps are a symptom and can recur. Try soda crackers, rice, bananas, potatoes, and flavored gelatins. Gelatins are especially good since they are made primarily of water.

Decaffeinated Tea
Just another tasty way to get fluids in your body. Don't drink caffeinated tea, however, as caffeine is a mild diuretic.

Electrolyte Drinks
To make your own fluid replacement, mix 4 teaspoons sugar and 1/2 teaspoon salt with 1 quart water. Mixing electrolytes (such as salt) with a form of glucose (sugar) helps the body to better absorb the nutrients.

Lime Juice
Add 1 teaspoon lime juice, a pinch of salt, and 1 teaspoon sugar to a pint of water. Sip the beverage throughout the day to cure mild dehydration.

Raisins
They're packed with potassium, a body salt lost during dehydration.

Salt
Most Americans get plenty of salt. But if you're experiencing symptoms of mild dehydration or heat injury, or you're just plain sweating a lot, make sure you replace your salt. Eat salty foods such as salted pretzels, salted crackers, or salty nuts.

Watery Fruits
Bananas are the number one fruit for rehydration, but watery fruits are a delicious and nutritious way to restore fluids. Try cantaloupe, watermelon, and strawberries. Watery vegetables such as cucumbers are good too.

ELECTRIC SHOCK

A storm can bring downed power lines; after a hurricane, a person wading or driving through standing water may encounter live electricity. Know how to both avoid electrocution and how to help someone who has been. Note that even if a person seems fine after a shock, they should be taken to the emergency room if at all possible to be evaluated, as they could have internal electrical burns.

PREVENTION

If your basement or house floods, don't wade through water where there are electric appliances. Don't wade through water to access a main power switch. Don't drive through standing water around downed power lines, and never touch a fallen power line yourself, even if it seems inactive. If an electrical appliance or tool has gotten wet, even if you think it is completely dry, it should be evaluated by someone with electrician's training before it is used again.

HELPING SOMEONE ELSE

If you see someone who has suffered an electric shock, do not endanger yourself when you try to help them. The current can move into you. You can try to move the source of the current away from them with a non-conductive material: cardboard and wood, for example, are not conductors. Plastic does not conduct electricity either. However, high-voltage power lines are not safe and should be handled by professionals only. Stay at least 20 feet away from them.

TREATMENT

Know CPR so you can perform it if necessary. Know how to treat burns with sterile bandages. The CDC warns against removing burned clothing.

FROSTBITE

You're caught outside unexpectedly—stranded by the roadside in winter, for example. One danger is frostbite and its lesser cousin, frostnip. Most people know that exposed skin can develop frostbite, the condition that occurs when skin and underlying tissue freeze. Frostbite can occur even in covered skin, however.

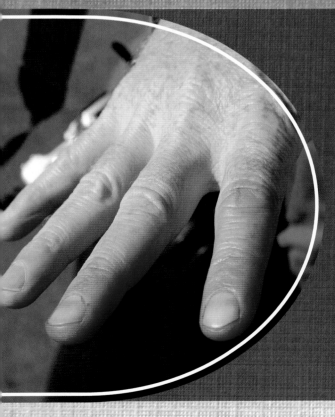

SYMPTOMS

If your exposed skin—often the ears, nose, and fingers—redden from cold, you're experiencing frostnip, a precursor to frostbite. When the skin turns white or yellow—or worse, progresses to black— it's an indication of frostbite. The skin may become prickly or numb, and hard. Eventually, frostbite affects not just the skin but the tissues underneath. Frostbite can set in quickly, especially if you touch ice or frozen metal.

PREVENTION

Dress appropriately for the weather. Invest in windproof and waterproof outer layers. On car trips, make sure you have a coat, hat, and gloves, even if you're driving for a short distance and expect your car heater to keep you warm. Hand and foot warmers can help as well. When you're getting dressed, remember that layers can help trap warmth near your body. Make sure hats fully cover your head and ears, since the tips of your ears are a common place for frostbite. And if you do get stranded in a cold place, don't drink alcohol to keep yourself warm: Drinking will in fact make you lose more heat.

TREATMENT

If someone in your group is affected by frostbite, it is important to warm them up quickly. Get them somewhere warm. If you can't get them somewhere warm immediately, do not try to thaw the skin—a repeated cycle of warmth and freezing can be more damaging. Ideally, the patient will not have to walk on frostbitten feet.

Once you are someplace warmer, remove wet clothing. Don't apply heat directly through a heating pad or by holding hands up a fire. Instead, warm the affected skin with warm—not hot—water for at least a half hour. If water is not available, use your breath. Don't rub the skin, which can damage it further. Sensation may be somewhat painful as it returns to the affected areas. Once the skin is warm again, loosely bandage the affected area, keeping fingers and toes separated from each other. If skin blisters, a common side effect, allow the blister to break on its own.

Over the counter pain medication can help.

If you can seek medical attention, do so as soon as possible. The patient might require debridement, the removal of dead tissue.

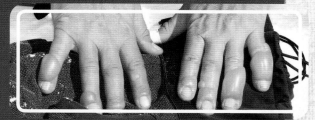

HEAT-RELATED ILLNESSES

While humans managed to live for millennia without air conditioning, modern humans have become acclimated to it. We treasure the ability to go from working in a hot garden to a cool place indoors. In a survival situation, however, air conditioning may no longer be available. And while feeling overheated can just be a matter of discomfort, it can also become a health matter, especially for any children or elderly folks in your group. The medical profession divides heat-related illnesses into three categories. From least to most severe, these are heat cramps, heat exhaustion, and heatstroke.

PREVENTION

A lot of problems can be staved off through prevention. If you're outside, or working indoors in a hot environment, make sure you are taking rest breaks where you hydrate. Stay in the shade, and wear a hat with a wide brim. Do not work outdoors during the hottest hours of the afternoon. Loose clothing in light colors will reflect the heat instead of absorbing it. Don't drink alcohol.

Never leave a baby or pet in a car. The temperature in a car can climb quickly, and heatstroke can result.

HEAT CRAMPS

Heat cramps, the mildest of the conditions, can happen when you exercise. If you experience muscle pain, cramps, or heavy sweating, it's a sign that your body is working too hard. Stop what you're doing and move to shade if you can. Drink water or other fluids, though nothing with caffeine or alcohol. Cramps that persist after an hour signal a need for medical attention if any is available.

HEAT EXHAUSTION

While heat exhaustion is not as serious as heatstroke, it is not something to dismiss. Keep a sharp eye on any children or elderly people in your group, as they are more vulnerable to heat exhaustion and may not recognize the symptoms. One symptom of heat exhaustion is actually counterintuitive: Skin can become cold and clammy rather than feeling hot, and pale rather than reddened. Goose bumps may even appear! Other symptoms include profuse sweating, dizziness or lightheadedness, muscle aches/cramps and headaches, a fast pulse, and nausea. If heat exhaustion persists, fainting or vomiting may occur. If you or someone in your group is experiencing these symptoms, stop any activity immediately. Move to a cool, shady place. Make sure clothes are  loose, and legs elevated above the heart. Hydrate by drinking water or a drink with electrolytes. (Do not drink anything with caffeine, alcohol, or excessive sugar.) If you can, prepare a cool shower or bath. If you're outside in nature, look for a pond or stream. If not, place cool, wet cloths on the skin. Symptoms that persist after 30 minutes to an hour signal a need for medical attention if at all possible.

Note that if you experience heat exhaustion, you may be more prone to experience it again. Even if you feel fine in the weeks that follow an episode of heat exhaustion, take it easy and watch carefully to see if symptoms reappear.

HEAT STROKE

When your body's temperature exceeds 103 degrees Fahrenheit, it is a medical emergency. Damage to the brain and other internal organs can happen. If you do not have a thermometer available to check someone's temperature, fainting, nausea, confusion and/or agitation, dizziness, and a fast pulse are all signs of heat stroke. Skin may be dry or damp, and hot to the touch. Skin may appear flushed. A person may have a headache. In some cases, seizures may occur.

The methods for helping someone with heatstroke in the short term are similar to helping someone with heat exhaustion: Get them to a shady, cool place and cool them down with water or ice packs. For best results, place the ice packs at the armpits, groin, neck, and back—however, do not use ice packs with very young or very old patients, or people with chronic ailments.

Loosen any clothing. Soaking sheets or towels in water and laying them over the patient can help. A cool shower or bath can help as well, but do not leave a person alone in case of fainting or confusion. If they are able to drink, help them sip water. And regardless of how well you are trained in first aid or how self-sufficient you are, unless you are in a survival situation where medical attention is not at all available, call for medical attention immediately.

As with heat exhaustion, even if the patient recovers from an episode, he or she may be more sensitive to heat and more likely to experience another episode in the weeks that follow.

HYPOTHERMIA

While our bodies do a pretty good job of regulating temperature, extremely hot and extremely cold conditions can both wreak havoc with our systems. When internal temperature drops below 95 degrees Fahrenheit, it can prove deadly. And to some people's surprise, hypothermia can occur even if the outside temperature is above the freezing point, particularly if a person is also wet (from rain or sleet) or chilled. You can even suffer from hypothermia indoors, if the temperature is below 50 degrees for a long period of time; babies in cold bedrooms have been known to suffer from hypothermia, for example, and older adults can also be at greater risk.

PREVENTION

Dress in warm layers in colder temperatures. Keep a blanket and spare warm clothes in the trunk of your car. Mittens tend to preserve body heat better than gloves; wearing a set of mittens over a pair of gloves if you're going to be outside for a longer period of time can provide a good balance between warmth and flexibility, as you can remove the mittens if you need to perform a task that requires manual dexterity. Have a plan for how to stay warm if the heating goes down.

SYMPTOMS

Slurred speech, drowsiness, and confusion are all hallmarks of hypothermia, as are numbness in the extremities and shivering. Infants, who are at greater risk than adults, may have bright red skin. Unconsciousness can follow.

TREATMENT

Like heatstroke, hypothermia is a medical emergency. If you can summon medical help, do so rather than trying to solve the problem yourself. While you wait, or if help is unavailable, get the patient under shelter and away from wind, preferably inside. Remove wet clothes, and try to warm the person gradually. Warm the person's trunk before their extremities—trying to warm their arms and legs without first warming the center of their body can actually cause shock. Warm blankets, warm clothing, and body heat can all help. Do not, however, immerse the person in a hot bath, as warming that is too rapid can cause an irregular heart rhythm. If a person is capable of drinking, warm beverages can help, though avoid alcohol. You can use chemical hot packs if you have any, but wrap them in towels first.

POISONOUS PLANT RASHES

Contact with poison ivy, poison oak, or poison sumac often goes hand in hand with outdoor activities. The problem stems from the plant's colorless oil, called urushiol. Whenever one of these plants is cut, crushed, stepped on, sat on, grabbed, rolled on, kicked, or disturbed, the oil is released. Once on the victim, the toxic oil penetrates the skin and a rash appears within 12 to 48 hours after exposure. This is a true allergic reaction to compounds in the urushiol. The rash starts as small bumps and progresses into enlarged, itchy blisters. No body part is immune to the oil, although areas most often irritated are the face, arms, hands, legs, and genitals.

DON'T TOUCH!

Touching the oil after initial contact is what spreads the rash—something easily done. For example, you unknowingly walk over poison ivy and the oily residue sticks like glue to your hiking boots. Later, you remove the boots, unwittingly touching the residue in the process. The oil easily spreads from the hands, to the face, and even to the genital area should you make the unfortunate decision to use the bathroom. The damage is done by the time the rash breaks out. Touching the rash once it appears does not spread the oil—or the rash.

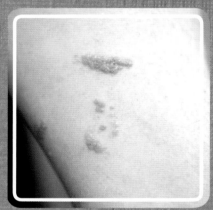

Warning! Since poison plant oils don't just disappear, it's crucial to wash anything that has had contact with the victim or the oil, including clothing, boots, pets, other people, sleeping bags, fishing poles, walking sticks, etc. Use gloves when cleaning pets, people, and objects that may have had contact with the oil. Outdoor expeditions need not be ruined if people learn to recognize the terrible threesome.

Here are some pointers:

• **Poison ivy.** Poison ivy plants have serrated, pointed leaves that appear in groups of three leaflets. The leaves are green in summer but are reddish in spring and fall. Their appearance can vary, and poison ivy plants are found everywhere in the United States. In the East, Midwest, and South, it grows as a climbing vine. In the West and northern states, poison ivy resembles a shrub. Poison ivy rarely appears above 5,000 feet.

• **Poison oak.** Like poison ivy, poison oak has leaves of three, and the shrub's size differs depending on location. In the Southeast, it appears as a small shrub, while in the West, poison oak appears as a large shrub. It has greenish-white berries and oaklike leaves.

• **Poison sumac.** The leafy one of this threesome is poison sumac, a small shrub with two rows of 7 to 13 leaflets. Sumac prefers the swampy bogs of northern states and swamps in southern states. Its leaves are smooth-edged and remain red; the plant has cream-colored berries. Unlike poison ivy and oak, poison sumac does not produce leaves in groups of three.

SIMPLE REMEDIES

Aloe vera

According to folk medicine, aloe vera sap helps treat poison ivy rash through its anti-inflammatory constituents. Grow a plant in your home or rooftop garden, so you can easily break off a leaf and apply the sap to the affected area. Allow to dry and gently wash off. Reapply every two hours.

Baking Soda

Concoct a paste of baking soda and water, and spread it on the affected area. Freshen the application every two hours for a total of three applications each day. Before going to bed, pour a cup of baking soda into a lukewarm bath and take a soak.

Coffee

If you have any leftover (cold) coffee in your cup, pouring it on a poison ivy rash may be a good way to get rid of the coffee and the rash. Appalachian folk medicine followers believe in washing the affected area with a cup of cold black coffee. Coffee beans contain chlorogenic acid, an anti-inflammatory.

Soap and Water

Waste no time in getting the poisonous plant victim in contact with soap and water. Quickly, but gently, wash the affected area with lukewarm water and mild, plain soap. Air-dry the skin. Any towels used for cleaning should be washed immediately in hot water and detergent since the oil can linger.

Cover Up

When working and playing outdoors in prime poisonous plant territory, wear long pants, long-sleeved shirts, protective footwear, and if gardening, gloves. Remember the pet connection. Often a mysterious case of rash can be traced to the furry family member who diligently patrols the outdoors: Fido or Fluffy. The oil gets on the animal's fur and is transferred to you via petting.

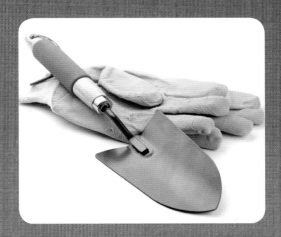

Debunking Myths

Myth: Burning poison ivy will get rid of it. False. Never burn poison ivy, especially in an enclosed environment such as a fireplace or firepit. The oil, urushiol, is carried in the smoke and can seriously irritate your eyes, skin, and lungs.

Myth: Dead plants don't give you a rash. False. Yes, they do. Even after a plant is dead, the oil lives on for years and can give you a rash.

Myth: The "leaves of three" motto always holds true. False. Never assume poison ivy and poison oak come with three leaves. Leaflets may come in groups of five, seven, or even nine.

Myth: Spring and summer are poison ivy/oak/sumac season. False. Urushiol, the oil that causes the reaction, doesn't take winters off. Even in colder months when the plants are bare, the twigs can still cause a powerful reaction.

SNAKE BITES

If you live in urban areas, you may be used to seeing snakes only at the zoo. However, even in urban areas, your chances of encountering snakes go up on times of crisis. Natural disasters like storms and hurricanes can displace snakes just as surely as they displace humans. If you return home after a crisis, be alert for snakes that may have entered your house. And be especially careful if you wade near standing water.

KNOW VENOMOUS SNAKES

While many North American snakes aren't dangerous, know and steer clear of these four in particular: rattlesnakes, coral snakes, water moccasins, and copperheads.

Western diamondback rattlesnake

Water moccasin

Eastern coral snake

Copperhead

DON'T CONFRONT, AVOID

If you see a snake, back away slowly rather than trying to trap it. If the snake has bitten you or someone else, pay close attention to its markings, which may help identify the type of snake and provide critical medical information. However, resist the temptation to try to capture the snake and further endanger yourself.

IF SOMEONE IS BITTEN

Snake bites can vary in severity, as can the symptoms that result. Pain at the bite site, nausea, and weakness are all common symptoms; vision can also be impaired. Seek medical attention if it's available. Keep the patient calm and still, seated or lying down. Ideally the wounded limb should be positioned above the heart. Clean the wound with soap and water, and apply a clean, dry dressing. Since swelling can occur, remove jewelry from any bitten area, as well as the shoe if a leg or foot was bitten.

WHAT NOT TO DO

If you have vague memories of treating snakebites from scouting trips years ago, jettison that knowledge. Current guidance differs significantly from past guidance. Specifically, do not attempt to put on a tourniquet to stop any venom from spreading. Never try to suck out the venom. Do not cut the wound to get the blood flowing more freely. Even if there is swelling, do not apply ice.

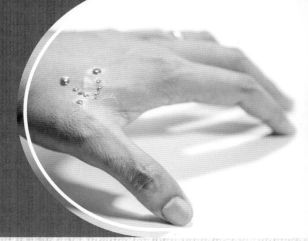

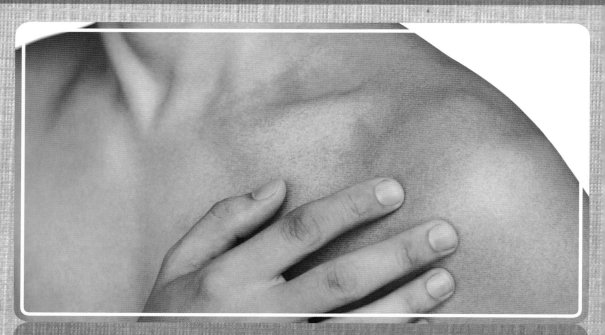

SUNBURN

A sunburn is one of the most common hazards of the great outdoors. By the time the skin starts to become red, the damage has been done. Pain isn't always instantly noticeable, either. You may feel like you're glowing after two hours without sun protection, but just wait awhile. You'll change your tune (not to mention color) when the pain sets in, typically 6 to 48 hours after sun exposure.

Like household burns, sunburns are summed up by degree. Mild sunburns are deep pink, punctuated by a hot, burning sensation. Moderate sunburns are red, clothing lines are prominent, and the skin itches and stings. Severe sunburns result in bright red skin, blisters, fever, chills, and nausea. Being burned to a crisp can lead to serious consequences later in life. In fact, one severe, blistering sunburn during childhood doubles your chances of developing melanoma, a potential deadly form of skin cancer.

Obviously, covering up and applying a waterproof sunscreen with a high SPF (sun protection factor) is the best way to prevent sunburn. However, if you don't have access to sunscreen, these home remedies should help.

WATER

As the sun fried your skin, it also dehydrated it. Be sure to replenish liquids by drinking plenty of water while recovering from a sunburn. Being well hydrated will help burns heal better. You'll know you're hydrated when your urine runs almost clear.

BAKING SODA

Adding a few heaping tablespoons of baking soda to cool bathwater makes a sunburn-soothing remedy. Just keep your soaking time down to 15 to 20 minutes. If you soak any longer, you risk drying out your already lizardlike skin. When you've emerged from the bath, resist the urge to towel off. Instead air-dry and don't wipe the baking soda off.

CHAMOMILE TEA

Brew dried chamomile in a tea and sponge onto affected areas. Make the tea by combining 1 teaspoon dried chamomile with 1 cup boiling water, or use a prepackaged chamomile tea bag. Cool and apply. Do not use chamomile if you have pollen allergies, or else you may suffer a skin reaction atop the burn.

MILK

Cool off with a cold glass of milk. Don't drink it; put it right on your body. Soak a facecloth in equal parts cold milk and cool water, wring it out, and gently press it on the burned areas.

OATMEAL

Oatmeal added to cool bathwater offers wonderful relief for sunburned skin. Fill up the bathtub with cool water, not cold water since that can send the body into shock. Scoop 1/2 to 1 cup oatmeal—an ideal skin soother—and mix it in. As with the baking soda, air-dry your body and don't wipe the oatmeal off your skin.

ALOE VERA

The thick, gel-like juice of the aloe vera plant can take the sting and redness out of a sunburn. Aloe vera causes blood vessels to constrict. Simply slit open one of the broad leaves and apply the gel directly to the burn. Apply five to six times per day for several days.

TICK BITES

You may not even know you've been bitten by a tick, as the majority of bites are painless and other symptoms such as redness and swelling can occur for a variety of reasons. Unfortunately, ticks can carry disease, specifically Lyme disease and Rocky Mountain spotted fever. Fortunately, it does take some time—scientists believe 36 hours—for ticks to transmit Lyme disease, although other diseases may only take a few hours. If you find a tick, don't panic or assume you have now contracted a disease.

PREVENTION

Give ticks fewer ways to bite you by wearing long sleeves and trousers as you walk through the woods. Light colors will show a tick better than dark colors. Tucking your trousers into your socks and shoes provides an extra measure of safety. When you return home, do a visual inspection for ticks, and run a fine-tooth comb through your hair.

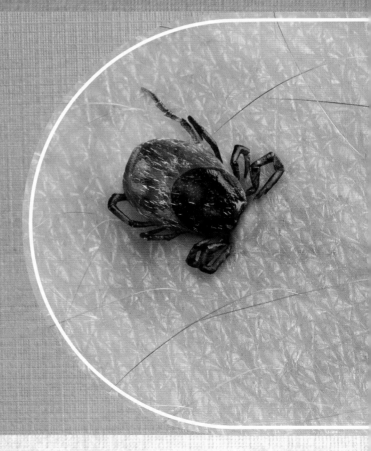

REMOVING A TICK

Tweezers can help you remove the tick whole, without leaving any parts behind. Hold the tick as close to your body as possible with the tweezers and gently, carefully, slowly remove it. Don't use your hands, and be careful of twisting the tick. Once you've removed it, preserve the tick by placing it in a small, alcohol-filled jar with a tight-fitting lid so that your doctor can test it should you develop signs of infection, such as a fever, lethargy, and/or a rash where the tick was attached.

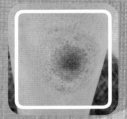

The rash caused by Lyme disease often has a distinctive bull's eye shape. It can develop in the weeks that follow the bite, so keep an eye out for a rash at the bite site for up to fourteen days.

WHAT NOT TO DO

The old folk method of removing ticks—burning them with a blown-out match—is not really very effective.

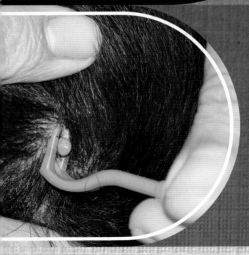

FURRY FRIENDS

Dogs can be a target of ticks, so examine them when you return home, not just yourself. Their ears can be a popular target, so watch for your dog pawing at its ears or indicating distress. As with humans, the best way to remove a tick is to use tweezers to grasp it firmly at skin level and pull it straight out with gentle, steady pressure. Keep in mind that you want to remove the entire tick intact.